Turenne

Henry Montague Hozier

BIBLIOLIFE

TURENNE.

HENRY DAVVERGNE VICOMTE DE TVRENNE

TURENNE.

TURENNE.

BY

H. M. HOZIER.

LONDON: CHAPMAN AND HALL,
LIMITED.

1885.

PREFACE.

VARIOUS works have appeared on the life of Turenne from the seventeenth century down to the present time—such as those by Buison, Ragunet, Grimoard, and Armagnac. More valuable than these are the *History of Turenne*, by Ramsay; Turenne's own *Memoirs*, and the *Memoirs* of the Duke of York, afterwards King James II. of England, who served for four years on the staff of the marshal, and for two years with Condé in the wars of the Fronde in the Spanish army.

The best criticism on the military operations of Turenne is, no doubt, that dictated by Napoleon at St. Helena, although this is inexact in minor points, such as dates and proper names, probably because the exiled Emperor at St. Helena had no good library to consult.

Within the last few weeks an excellent work on Turenne has been issued in Paris under the direction of Monsieur Georges Hartrel, written by Professor Rey.

It gives important extracts from the correspondence in
the public archives of France that has not before been
published, but is marred by being evidently written
with the object of flattering French national vanity,
and of stirring up a desire for a war of revenge
against Germany.

Yet these works, however valuable as historical
biographies and as admirable accounts of campaigns
and battles, do not throw up a vivid picture of the
aspect of war in the time of the great captain, or
give us those details of military administration and
organization which enable the student to trace the
development of military science during the seventeenth
century.

It requires a long and tedious research for isolated
facts through many books before we can learn how the
younger son of the Calvinist Duke of Bouillon rose
to the highest position in the armies of France in the
time of the greatest grandeur of the greatest of French
monarchs. It needs much labour and much reading
to enable us to trace how a stammering youth of so
sickly a disposition that he was considered in his
boyhood unfit for military service, and who would in
our days almost certainly be rejected by the medical
examiners for Sandhurst, rose to be the greatest of
the captains who commanded the armies even of
Lewis XIV.

Of Turenne's appearance in manhood we may judge from the picture by Mauzaisse, in the gallery of Versailles, or still better, probably, from the excellent picture by Seuin, dated 1670, in the Jones Collection at South Kensington. We find him awkward, broad-shouldered, short-necked, with rather dark hair, high complexion and morose countenance. But below this uncaptivating exterior, which to an inobservant eye would appear almost vulgar, there glowed a heart of gold, a will of iron, a determination of steel, and a mind infinite in resource.

The endeavour of the writer of this essay has been to form a connected story of his steady advance in life, to trace the various changes which he conducted in the science of war from the time that he was first made a marshal until he fell mortally wounded by a roundshot on the hill above the Salzbach.

An attempt also is made to explain why, early in the seventeenth century, cavalry was a predominant force in European armies; why sieges were as a rule the principal operations of war; why orders of battle were parallel; why armies intrenched themselves constantly instead of manœuvring in the open field; and how it came about that Turenne was the first to indicate an oblique formation for attack, which Frederick the Great afterwards developed on the battle-field, and Napoleon made an integral element of strategy; and how it was that in the latter part of the seventeenth century the armies of Lewis XIV., organized by Louvain, led by Turenne or Luxembourg, made that great stride in scientific warfare which divides the cumbrous procedure of the middle ages from the startling enterprise and exhaustive combinations that mark the strategy of Napoleon or Moltke.

We would, too, trace how the bodyguard of Henry IV. was gradually increased and improved, until in 1672 Lewis XIV. was able to take the field with an army of over 200,000 men, and how armies composed at the beginning of the century of two-thirds cavalry became altered in their constitution, until in later years the infantry formed three-fourths of the fighting columns.

We must strive to solve why, under Turenne, French armies for the first time made marches which might be dignified as manœuvres; how it was that his confidence and boldness increased in each succeeding year; why, as Napoleon remarks, Turenne was the only general whose courage gained force as his experience increased; how, different from the ordinary leaders of his day, he did not look upon war as a mere succession of battles and sieges, but trusted much to movements and marches, and thence gained such great results that a contemporary soldier declared that he would wish at the end of a battle to be with Condé, at the end of a campaign with Turenne.

From his time and from his tuition arose the strategical aptitude of the army of France. Napoleon, who gave Turenne's body a tomb under the dome of the Invalides, devoted to Turenne's memory his own dying thoughts. At St. Helena he wrote a sketch of Turenne's campaigns, and accompanied it with critical observations. When his spirit was slowly flitting away the name of Turenne was still upon his lips, and in bidding farewell to the few friends who surrounded him he said, " I am going to rejoin Kléber, Desaix, Lannes, Masséna, Bessières, Duroe, Ney. . . . They will come to meet me ; they will feel once again the intoxication of human glory. . . . We shall talk of what we have done . . . . we shall talk of our art with Frederic, Turenne, Condé, Cæsar, Hannibal." It was a grand homage to the greatest soldier of the armies of the Monarchy from the greatest soldier of the armies of the Revolution.

CONTENTS.

CHAPTER VII.

CHAPTER VIII.

CHAPTER IX.

CHAPTER X.

CHAPTER XI.

CHAPTER XII.

CHAPTER XIII.

TURENNE.

CHAPTER I.

EDUCATION.

HENRY DE LA TOUR D'AUVERGNE, VISCOUNT TURENNE, was born at Sedan on the 11th September, 1611. He was the second son of Henry de la Tour d'Auvergne, Duke of Bouillon, sovereign prince of Sedan, and of Elisabeth of Nassau, daughter of William I. of Nassau, Prince of Orange. On his father's side he sprang from the ancient Counts of Auvergne, and thus was connected with the greatest families of Europe. On his mother's side he was descended from that grand house of Nassau which has given an emperor to Germany, many captains-general to Holland, and a king to England. William, first of the name, Prince of Orange Nassau, Stadtholder of Holland, grandfather of Turenne, had headed the revolt of the United Provinces against Spain. His son Maurice, uncle of Turenne, had been captain-general of the states, and by extraordinary abilities had raised himself almost to kingly power, though much dreaded and opposed by a jealous municipal oligarchy. In 1650 William II.

B

died childless, and his power was dissolved; but a few
days after his death his widow, Mary, daughter of
Charles I. of England, gave birth to a son who became an
opponent worthy of Turenne, saved Holland from slavery,
curbed the power of France, and established a free
constitution in England. Turenne was six years younger
than his elder brother, Frederick Maurice, Prince of
Sedan, afterwards Duke of Bouillon, who exercised considerable influence on many events of his life. His father
was the friend and companion in arms of Henry of
Navarre, the first Bourbon King of France. Bouillon had
defended his master bravely on fields of battle against the
Guises and the Leaguers, and had taken an important
part in the weightiest negotiations with England, Germany,
and the United Provinces. A prominent leader of the
Calvinist party, as much from his mental attainments,
remarkable in that age, as through his rare political and
military qualities, he naturally educated his two sons in
his own religion.

Turenne received the usual education of a young
nobleman of the time who was destined for any other
profession than that of the Church. His studies were
philosophy, history, mathematics, Italian, dancing, tennis,
horsemanship, and hunting. Tradition, however, tells that
he was not happy with philosophical books, and that when
a boy his intellectual faculties were not nearly so brilliant
as those of the dashing son of Condé, who was one day to
be his great rival. Of a shy and timid disposition, to
which a pronounced stutter contributed, he was slow in
mind, learnt with difficulty, and was repelled by the cruel
corporal punishments which in those days were bestowed
upon the schoolboy with equal hand, whether peasant or
prince. His father, of a broader mind than his severe

teachers, took another course; he appealed to the boy's honour, and so led him on to steady work, and to considerable progress even in the classical philosophy which he cordially detested. Although he looked with aversion upon mathematics and ethics, he read with avidity the works of Cæsar, of Quintus Curtius, and the history of Alexander the Great. So high stood his admiration for the Macedonian hero, that he challenged to a duel an officer who one day scoffed at the stories of this conqueror's campaigns as incredible romances.

The thirst with which he devoured military history showed a natural military taste. But he was feeble and delicate in early boyhood. His father believed, and expressed his belief, that he never would be able to bear the hardships of war. To prove the reverse, Turenne, at ten years of age it is said, determined to pass a winter's night on the ramparts of Sedan, and in cold weather, was found asleep on a gun-carriage upon the parapet. This convinced the duke, his father, of his determination of character, and also of the impossibility of placing him in any other profession than that which the boy himself had resolved to adopt.

It is said that in his youth he displayed the reserved and thoughtful disposition which pre-eminently distinguished him in after life above the rude soldiers and frivolous courtiers of his time. It was natural that the son of a father who had fought in the Protestant cause should imbibe some of the Puritan feeling that then was so pronounced in Northern Europe, and it is stated that even in early boyhood he showed a cold and reserved character, a superiority of reason over imagination, a sincere love of truth, and an exquisite sensibility of pity towards the unfortunate. These characteristics were certainly developed

in later life. It is said that even when a child he distributed his pocket-money among the poor, and divided
his own food with his companions.

When the boy was twelve years old his father died.
His education was continued by his mother, who was more
Protestant than his father. Now he discarded book learning almost entirely, and devoted himself nearly exclusively
to physical exercises, which improved his constitution, and
made him more capable of bearing military fatigue. At
fourteen years of age he was sent to Holland to learn the
rudiments of the art of war under his uncle, Maurice of
Nassau, who was justly considered one of the greatest
captains of the century.

This was in 1625. More than a century had passed
since Luther had appeared before the Diet of Augsburg,
and had promulgated the opinions which shook to their
foundations the ancient religious observances of the west.
The spirit of reform had penetrated into the low countries.
These lay politically under the dominion of Spain, spiritu-
ally under that of Rome. Yet, notwithstanding perse-
cution, opinions opposed to those authorised by Rome
continually developed there. It was in vain that Philip II.
sent the intelligent Margaret of Parma, aided by her
enlightened minister, Granvelle, to govern these countries.
The people had revolted to defend their privileges, and the
insulted nobility had joined in the war. It was in vain
that Margaret had been replaced by the stern Duke of
Alva. Neither conciliation nor severity had sufficed to
reduce a tiny population struggling under the shelter of
their dykes for liberty of conscience. The barbarities
of Alva only determined them to establish political
independence in order to guarantee religious liberty.

William of Orange founded the republic of the United

Provinces, and as stadtholder, admiral-general, and captain-general, was the guiding genius of this rising state until Gerard assassinated him. His son, Maurice of Nassau, avenged his father. Elected President of the Council of State of the United Provinces immediately after the murder of William, he justified the opinion which had been formed of his talent. He spared no exertion, no sacrifice, no care, to maintain the strife against the detested despotism of Spain. Severe discipline was established among his troops, exact order imparted to his military administration. He fell suddenly upon the Spanish army of occupation while Alexander Farnese was supporting in France the party of the League against Henry of Navarre. He took from the Spaniards many towns, concluded at the Hague an offensive and defensive alliance with France and England, and stamped his reputation as a great general by the splendid defence of Ostend, of which the siege cost the Master of the Escurial 60,000 men. Discouraged by such dogged endurance Spain signed, in 1609, a truce of twelve years. Europe was surprised that a monarch, master of the treasures of the new world, should fail to reduce a tiny republic in extent little superior to the principality of Wales. From Edinburgh to Vienna, from Stralsund to La Rochelle, those rejoiced greatly who were eager for religious liberty. To them a valuable lesson was given. They saw, clearly shown before their eyes, that in an unhallowed cause treasures, reputation, grand armies, talented generals, and indefatigable administrators may be exhausted, but constancy and faith in a just endeavour, although hampered by poverty and exposed apparently to every disadvantage, had not been borne down.

To us, who can judge from the light of subsequent history, it does not appear so remarkable that the Spanish

power, which had risen to within a reasonable distance of
absolute dominion under Charles V., should have fallen so
low as to have been defied by the United Provinces. In
England alone, in the seventeenth century, the wise
policy was followed by which the parliament of the realm
should take its stand firmly on its constitutional right to
give or withhold money and resolutely to refuse funds for
the support of armies, unless ample securities had been
provided against despotism. In Spain, where parliamentary institutions had been as strong as any that ever
sat at Westminster, the Cortes struggled indeed for this
constitutional principle, but struggled too late. The
mechanics of Toledo, the citizens of Valladolid, eventually
fought in vain for the privileges of the Castillian Cortes
against the veteran battalions of Charles V. Eventually,
too, in the next generation, the burghers of Saragossa rose
against Philip II. for the old constitution of Aragon.
But it was too late. Absolute power had already passed
into the hands of the Prince, and under the withering and
blighting effect of that absolute power the real power of
the state decayed as though struck with palsy.

At the beginning of the seventeenth century, Spain, as
a formidable empire, was already declining. From that
time she ever decayed, though she never absolutely fell
till Napoleon planted his heel upon her neck. She still
held in Europe the provinces of Milan, the two Sicilies,
Belgium, and Franche-Comté. Beyond the Atlantic her
dominions still spread on both sides of the equator far
beyond the limits of the torrid zone : but she was no
longer the Spain of Charles V. or Philip II., no longer the
Spain which had sent out the seamen of the Armada or
the soldiery of St. Quentin.

The truce between the Spanish Government and the

United Provinces expired in 1621. The monarchy was weaker, the republic stronger, than at its conclusion. Holland had increased its wealth and resources. The narrow countries round the Zuyder Zee which form the Batavian territory had been wrung from the waves, and were held against them by the art of man. Although its full industrial and commercial activity was not developed till after the peace of Westphalia, the respite of eleven years from Spanish war had allowed it to make progress which, in that age, was justly regarded as stupendous. As shown by Macaulay, it was a busy and populous hive in which new wealth was every day created, and masses of old wealth hoarded. The comforts of life, the cultivation of the soil, the commercial activity of Holland were far superior to that of England. Its countless canals, its whirling mills, crowded fleets of barges, constant succession of great towns, ports bristling with thousands of masts, large and stately mansions, trim villas, summer-houses and tulip-beds, produced on English travellers in that day an effect similar to that which the first sight of England now produces on a traveller from Colorado or Manitoba.

Hostilities at once began on the close of the truce. Soon the Spaniards lost all hope of success during the lifetime of Maurice of Nassau. He was a prince of admirable judgment, extraordinary bravery, consummate prudence and majestic air, born, as Ramsay says, with all the qualities necessary to found a republic, discipline an army, and control a people.

To the school of this captain the widowed Duchess of Bouillon sent Turenne. Maurice received the lad with kindly sympathy, questioned him to discover his character and habits, and resolved to treat him with the same

military severity as had been shown to his elder brother,
the Prince of Sedan. A musket was placed in his hands,
and Turenne served as a private soldier before even being
raised to the rank of non-commissioned officer. To this
excellent method of military training some of his subsequent success may have been due. The result of great
battles often depends upon an officer's knowledge of the
most minute military details. Turenne understood this
need, and cheerfully entered the army in the humblest of
its grades. To his mind there was nothing low, nothing
painful in handling a musket, in falling into the ranks, or
in rendering strict obedience to his captain, who, as it
happened, was a vassal of his brother's house. His education under Maurice of Nassau suddenly ceased. Death
deprived him of his uncle, and Henry Frederick of Nassau
succeeded his brother in the government of the United
Provinces and in the command of the army. He shortly
afterwards promoted his nephew, and Turenne rose to the
rank of a captain of infantry.

   The wars in the Low Countries at this period doubtless
gave excellent lessons in the details of military life, in the
interior economy of regiments, in the posting of guards,
the reconnoitring of roads and such minor exercises, but
manœuvres were practically unknown. The operations of
a campaign were confined almost entirely to the siege or
relief of towns, around which the contending forces were
cumbrously pivoted. As was the custom of the day,
armies separated in the autumn, and dispersed into winter
quarters. The soldiers were broken up into cantonments,
and the officers went on leave of absence.

   Turenne, every winter, came to France, where he was
admitted to Court, and continued his lessons in dancing
and accomplishments. Being only a younger son, he was

obliged to exercise care against the excessive expenses of the capital, and so early as the age of fifteen we find him, like another great soldier the Duke of Wellington, with a horror of debt, regulating his life with perfect order, intent on not exceeding his pecuniary resources, and denying himself many things, so as to need little for himself and to be able to bestow much upon others.

In these years he resisted with firmness, rare at his age, all the entanglements and temptations which a lax and glittering Court could offer him, and constantly showed that force of character and will of which during his life he gave many proofs. No doubt his scatheless passage through these temptations was due in some part to his Calvinist education ; but the standard set up by such an education was probably too severe to endure, and the unreasoning religious bitterness which had been imbued in his mind in early years, no doubt led to the reaction in later life which led him to embrace the Catholic creed, after constant intercourse with Catholic statesmen and Catholic soldiers had shown him that many nursery tales of the inherent wickedness of Rome were unfounded, unjust and uncharitable.

In the field he devoted himself strictly to military duties. His company was renowned as the best drilled and the best disciplined in the army. He did not trust its administration, as was the custom with well-born captains, to his lieutenant. He himself drilled the soldiers, instructed them patiently, and corrected them softly. He required from his men not only military discipline, but perfect moral regularity. He won their respect and affection by kindness, and denied himself necessaries in order to bestow comforts liberally upon them. Nor did he confine himself to improving the condition of his own

company alone.   He was equally kind to the soldiers of
other battalions, and became devotedly loved throughout
the whole force.

Henry Frederick renewed the offensive and defensive
alliance with France, and began a campaign against the
Spaniards.   Spinola was the general of Philip III., and
bravely defended his sovereign's cause against the House
of Orange.   It was a grand opportunity for a young
soldier.   Turenne saw two adversaries of great resource
and great intelligence pitted against each other.   He
took part in the principal expeditions made by Henry.
He was present at the sieges of Klundert, Wilhelmstadt
and Groll.   Everywhere he was an attentive observer.
He studied the operations.   He made inquiries from
officers,· engineers, sappers, and private soldiers.   He
despised all dangers in order to obtain accurate information.   When the siege of Hertogenbosch, otherwise
named Bois-le-Duc, was begun by the ' Dutch, he had
acquired, through a careful study of three years, a superior
knowledge of military necessities.

Hertogenbosch, the capital of the province of Northern
Brabant, lay at the confluence of the Dommel and of the
Aa, in a country easy to inundate.   It was a place of
great importance, as it covered the passages of the Meuse.
It was of great strength, and almost inaccessible on
account of the waters which, let loose to form an inundation, covered the surrounding country.   It was surrounded
with strong walls, furnished with heavy bastions, and protected by broad and deep ditches.   The approaches were
defended by several redoubts, and four bastioned forts
planted on the principal avenues.   It had been besieged
several times, but had never been taken, and was calculated to form an excellent base of operations for which·

ever of the belligerent armies should become its master.
The Dutch were prepared to make every effort to secure
such a vantage-point. The Spaniards were determined to
exhaust every military resource before yielding it. Here
Turenne for the first time was to distinguish himself in
active war. Here, according to his own testimony, he
learnt from his uncle the principles of choosing a camp
and attacking a fortress. The governor was a man of
great skill and consummate experience, but his garrison
consisted of only 2,300 infantry and four companies of
cavalry. He succeeded in drawing in 800 additional
men from the garrison of Breda, and in expelling from the
town all except those capable of bearing arms. The
Prince of Orange had under his command 36,000 soldiers.
After investing the fortress, the Prince assured his own
camp, as was the custom of the day, by lines of circumvallation, and with broad and steep ditches which he filled
with water by turning the rivers that washed the town.
He made his dispositions to attack the outworks from
four different points. Turenne followed with attentive
care every arrangement, and whenever not on duty went
to important points to make observations on the progress
of the siege. His worth as a soldier seems to have been
appreciated, for delicate duties were frequently entrusted
to him. He appears often to have been in the trenches.
He was chosen to establish the battery of six 24-pounders
which fired the first rounds. He was employed to storm
some posts and to drive back reconnoitring parties from
Breda which endeavoured to annoy the besiegers or in-
terrupt their convoys. Favourable reports must have
been made to the commander-in-chief of the way in
which he performed his duties, and of his personal bravery,
since the Prince of Orange, while he blamed the reckless

courage which Turenne exhibited, and which was one day
to prove fatal to him, told the officers of his staff that he
was much mistaken if the young man would not be a
great captain.

The siege was carried on with skill and vigour ; the
governor held out stoutly, but was at length forced to
capitulate after four months of resistance.   He obtained
from his conqueror all the honours which his bravery
deserved.

Turenne then left Holland for France, since in a country
where war was confined to sieges he could learn little more
than the art of pitching a camp, of attacking a fortress or
of defending one.   This was not enough for his ambition.
He wished to see war in all its phases, and desired to
serve in the armies of France, where he could find a more
varied school ; for though French armies still looked upon
the capture or relief of fortified towns as the great object
of campaigns, they operated over larger areas, and made
longer marches than a theatre such as Holland, intersected with perpetual canals and constant lagoons, could
afford.

Cardinal Richelieu gave him an opportunity to gratify
his longing which he himself could hardly have anticipated.

The two great ministers who swayed the destinies of
France during the reign of Lewis XIII. and the minority
of Lewis XIV. found it incumbent upon them to establish
the supremacy of the crown over the nobility.

In France there had been no Wars of the Roses as in
England.   The great houses had not broken each other
up by civil warfare as in this country, and at the beginning
of the seventeenth century were oppressors of the people
and dangerous to the king.   The difference between the
two countries was due to a difference of military armament.

Heavy men-at-arms well mounted on stalwart horses formed, till after the invention of gunpowder, the fighting bodies of French armies. These were necessarily found from the nobility. In England the archers for many years before had been the most formidable element of a combatant force. The archer was a yeoman or a peasant. Hence the yeomanry and peasantry were integral portions of the chivalry of our island, made themselves respected in peace as well as war, and founded a powerful middle class which was able to assert its rights, and in the Wars of the Roses to curb the strength of the nobility. Men who do not credit a supreme guidance of apparently insignificant incidents might logically hold that our liberties, our rights, our maritime supremacy, our commercial preponderance, our Empire of India, and our extensive colonies, are due to the geological accident that the yew tree grows in luxuriant clusters on the chalk downs of Hampshire and of Dorset.

Such powerful houses as those of Lorraine, Bouillon, Enghien, and Longueville, nominally vassals of the crown, were practically independent sovereigns. In their fortified *châteaux*, they ground down the peasantry of their vast estates, and defied the edicts of the sovereign in the capital. To gain some liberty and some independence of life for the people, it was necessary that the crown should bring the nobles under control. These were not prepared to yield without a struggle. It required the iron hand of Richelieu, the subtle dexterity of Mazarin, the wars of the Fronde, and the organization of Louvois before the policy begun by Henry IV. could be carried out and the nobility of France reduced to the position of a subject estate. Nor then was the object which had been in part originally intended achieved. The nobility were indeed controlled, but the liberties of the commons were swept away in the struggles that led to the curtailment of the privileges of the nobles.

In the monarchies of the Middle Ages the power of the sword belonged to the prince, but the power of the purse to the nation. As progress and civilization made the sword of the prince more and more formidable to the nation the purse of the nation became more and more necessary to the prince. His hereditary revenues would no longer suffice even for the expense of civil government. It was impossible that without a regular and extensive system of taxation he could keep in constant efficiency a body of disciplined troops or of mercenary levies.

The parliamentary assemblies of the Continent failed to enforce their constitutional right to give or withhold money, and when under Lewis XIV. great military establishments were formed in France, no new securities for public liberty were devised. Consequently the old parliamentary institutions which had always been feeble, languished, and died of mere weakness, and the people and the nobility sank together under the despotism of the monarch.

When the young Turenne returned to France from the capture of Hertogenbosch, Richelieu was engaged in the policy of curbing the nobility, and was watching with jealousy the house of Bouillon. The father of Turenne, head of that house at the very beginning of the century (1602), had been concerned in the conspiracy of Biron. A few years later, in 1605, he had openly endeavoured to raise the Calvinists in the name of their religious interests, and had almost placed Sedan in the position of a fortress hostile to the crown. Under Lewis XIII. the Duke of Bouillon had joined the party of the nobility against Concini, who then was attached to Marie de Medicis, out of hatred to the constable of Luynes. The very position of Sedan itself lying in the valley of the Meuse, on the frontiers of Luxembourg, made it an important strategical point, very desirable for the crown to hold, and very dangerous to the king if in unfriendly keeping. The crown was engaged in the attempt to reduce the nobles; these, when imperilled, sought alliances with the dukes of Lorraine, or of Bouillon, who could at Nancy and Sedan furnish them with easy and sure retreats. Richelieu, to break up these vantage posts of his opponents, sent an army into Lorraine to seize the principal places in the duchy, and made the Duchess Dowager of Bouillon sign a treaty by which she undertook to remain always attached to the interests of the king of France, who on his side engaged himself to protect her house.

Shortly after the signature of this treaty, the cardinal intended to place a garrison in Sedan. The duchess, informed of this project, recalled Turenne from Holland, and sent him into France as a hostage of her fidelity to the engagements which she had contracted. She thus hoped to save the sovereign rank of her elder son, and for a short time her policy succeeded, but finally the young duke drew upon himself the loss of his duchy by foolish endeavours to secure it. Then the glory of Turenne saved his life, but not his principality. This, however, did not occur till fourteen years after the siege of Hertogenbosch.

CHAPTER II.

THIRTY YEARS' WAR.

AT the Court of Lewis XIII. Turenne was welcomed on
account of both his birth and reputation. Received with
marked distinction by the king and by Richelieu, although
only nineteen years old, he was entrusted with the command of a regiment of infantry. In the administration of
his regiment he showed the same care as in that of his
company in Holland, and soon gained the congratulations of
the sovereign and of the cardinal on the state of his corps.

In September, 1630, he writes : "My regiment passed
to-day before the king, who has found it very fine, and
said it was in as good order as his own guards. He inspected
company by company, and after the inspection ordered me
to get into his carriage to go to the queen-mother, who
also told me that the king was much pleased with my
regiment, as was the cardinal too."

Nor was this care thrown away, for he was soon to be
called into active service, and to appear on the various
theatres of war, where French armies fought under the
directions of Richelieu, from the Rhine to the Pyrenees,
from the Alps to the Scheldt, in Lorraine, in Italy, and
in Spain.

Richelieu had formed a determined plan, which he had followed with unswerving steadiness since 1625, and which he has described in his correspondence. As he himself wrote to Lewis XIII. : "When your majesty entrusted me with the guidance of your counsels and with your confidence in the direction of affairs, the Huguenots divided the state with the crown, the nobility acted as though they were not subjects, and the governors of provinces as though they were sovereign princes ; foreign alliances were despised, private interests preferred to public. I promised your majesty to use all my industry and energy to ruin the Huguenot party, to reduce the pride of the nobility, to bring all subjects to a sense of their duty, and to raise the name of the French crown among foreign nations to the position that it ought to hold."

To gain the aid of the burghers against the nobility, and to obtain some sort of national approval of his policy, Richelieu assembled at the Tuileries, at the end of 1626, an assembly of notables, composed not only of princes and dukes, but of magistrates, clergy, representatives of the lower *noblesse*, and of burghers. Important questions were there brought forward, financial, military, commercial, and judicial. The cardinal was authorised to raise and maintain a standing army of 30,000 men. Then, when the post of Constable and Grand Admiral had been suppressed, when the minister had been given the title of Superintendent of Marine and Commerce, when the necessary funds had been voted which would allow France to place forty-five vessels of war upon the sea and to furnish ports to receive them, the assembly separated. With authority thus strengthened, Richelieu pursued his great designs with the determination of a hero and the vigour of a reformer. Without mercy, as without fear, he first struck

c

down the Huguenots, and made it impossible for them
again to become an armed party in the state. As yet they
were left their liberty of conscience and their equality
of citizenship.

To reduce the nobles he strained the forms and traditions of justice, pronounced sentence of death on his
opponents by commissioners chosen by himself, and let
neither degree nor birth shield those who were guilty of
infraction of law.

In foreign politics he took up again the great policy of
Henry IV., the key-note of which was to raise France by
degrading the house of Austria both in Spain and Germany. The immediate result of Richelieu's policy was the
elevation of France, the degradation of Spain, the religious
liberty of northern Germany, and great glory to the French
nation. Its development and outcome, after many years,
was the establishment of French preponderance over neighbouring countries, the victories of the First Napoleon, and
finally the battle of Sedan and the loss of Alsace. His
policy was a perpetual struggle to stay the course of the
progress of Spain, a determination that France should not
stand on the defensive, but should open passages by which
French armies could penetrate neighbouring states and aid
these to shake off Spanish domination. He dearly longed
to become powerful on the seas, since the sea gives entry
to every state. He wished to fortify Metz, advance on
Strasbourg, and there to gain an entry into Germany. He
would have planted a mighty fortress on the Swiss frontier
to overawe the cantons, and aimed at holding Geneva as
an outpost of France; Savoy and the country round the
sources of the Po, he wished to gain as an outlet into Italy;
Navarre and Franche-Comte he considered as naturally
and geographically portions of France itself.

French authors now wish to explain that this policy was
a policy directed solely against Austria and not against
Germany ; that it aimed at the abasement of a family, not
of a nation ; and was only intended to allow French armies
to penetrate into various regions to defend against Austria
the states which she was oppressing, such as the Dutch
and the Grisons, the Protestant princes of Germany, who
had been worsted in the first part of the Thirty Years'
War by Ferdinand II. ; Catalonia, of which the privileges
were being suppressed by Spanish centralization ; and
Portugal, which had lost her independence since the time
of Philip II. These assert that the foreign policy of
Richelieu in 1625 was justified by a situation which
France had not created, and which must be altered as
soon as possible if Western Europe was not to be trampled
under the feet of the Emperor.

There is much to be said from this point of view.
Germany at this time formed less a state than a con-
federacy of territories. Ferdinand II. was the most
powerful emperor who had sat on the throne of the
Hapsbourgs since Charles V., and was practically supported
by the whole power of Spain. It was supposed that he
contemplated a restoration of the ancient Roman Empire.
Yet those who calmly review the whole circumstances of
the situation, without going so far as Voltaire, who holds
that Richelieu merely made wars to make himself necessary,
can see little in the policy of Richelieu but a determination
to exchange for the supremacy of Spain in Europe the
supremacy of France.

When Turenne joined the service of France in 1629 the
first period of the Thirty Years' War was just concluded.
The northern provinces of Germany were plunged in
terror. Ferdinand in reckless abuse of his victory had

launched the famous Edict of Restitution, which decreed
that all Protestants should dispossess themselves of any
ecclesiastical property which had been secularised since
1555. The execution of the decree had been entrusted to
the soldiery of Tilly and of Wallenstein. The Fatherland
had fallen into the lowest abyss of misery. Never had a
country been handed over by its nominal sovereign to
armies so barbarous and so rapacious. It was generally
believed that the emperor wished to extend an absolute
monarchy over all Germany, and that the restoration of
Catholicism was but a pretext for the ambition of the
house of Austria.

The policy of Ferdinand appeared to be expressed in the
words of Wallenstein when he said, " There is no further
need of electors, nor of princes ; as in France and in Spain
there is only one king, so Germany should have but a
single master."

Ferdinand not content with threatening the states of
the north and the liberties of Germany, interfered in Italy,
where the question of succession to the rich duchies of
Mantua had arisen. A French prince, the Duke of Nevers,
and an Italian prince who was supported by Ferdinand
II., Philip IV., and Charles Emmanuel of Savoy, contended
for this possession.

The Spaniards besieged Casale. Richelieu struck a blow
against Spain. In the time between his capture of
Rochelle and the submission of Languedoc he sent an expedition over the Alps and raised the siege. After the
pacification with the Huguenots at Alais he again turned
his attention to Italy, obtained possession of the fortress of
Pinerolo and of Chambery, and forced the confederates to
make the treaty of Cherasco, which guaranteed the independence of the Duke of Nevers and compelled the Duke

of Savoy to give up to the French Pinerolo and the
passage of the Alps. At the same time he raised the
Swedes against the Empire, and by sending an army into
Lorraine against its duke, Charles IV., he prepared a road
into Germany by which he might strike the house of
Austria directly.

Turenne took part in the expedition sent to succour
Casale in 1630 under Schomberg, but on the appearance of
a French army before the place the Spaniards agreed to
peace, and hence there was no opportunity of seeing
service. During the following years until 1634 he appears to have divided his time between Paris and Holland.
In the latter country he took part in the campaigns of
Frederick Henry, his uncle, against Count Berghen, the
successor of Spinola. There, as in Italy, he served for
France, since the Dutch had concluded with Lewis XIII.
the treaty of Compiegne in 1624, and that of the Hague in
1630, by which France engaged to furnish to the Dutch
subsidies although not soldiers. While engaged in
Holland he followed with anxiety the march of Gustavus
Adolphus, and noted with joy the losses that the hero of
Sweden inflicted on Tilly. At the camp of Bergues he was
chosen to assist in an attack against a corps of 6,000
Spaniards who had sallied from Antwerp with 100 boats.
So great was the success of this expedition, that it was
compared to the taking of Bois le Duc.

During his campaigns in Holland he devoted himself to
study, and increased his knowledge in that school of
brilliant officers which surrounded the Prince of Orange.

In the war against Lorraine, Turenne for the first time
actively fought in the ranks of France. There under
Le Force he distinguished himself by his brilliant military
qualities. Charles IV. of Lorraine, as much through

instability of character as by zeal for the house of
Austria, passed his life in violating the contracts which
he made with Lewis XIII. He conspired with Gaston
intriguing at the court of the emperor ; vain and without
ballast, sometimes he appeared to resign himself to the
peace which he had signed. Anon he became indignant at
his humiliation. Loved by his people, he could, even
after the loss of Nancy, have obtained for France better
terms if he had been capable of a sustained effort, but
when he learnt that Richelieu wished to break the
marriage of his sister Margaret of Lorraine with Gaston,
and that the Parliament had been ordered to proceed
against her and her accomplices, the princes of his house,
in great perplexity he abdicated on the 19th January,
1634. He then retired into Alsace with 800 horsemen
and 2,000 infantry, leaving the duchies of Lorraine and
Bar to his brother, the Cardinal Nicholas, hoping that
the emperor would place him at the head of the imperial
armies. Richelieu refused to accept the abdication as
serious, and prepared to seize the two fortresses of Bitche
and La Motte. Marshal de la Force besieged La Motte,
and the regiment of Turenne was amongst those ordered
for this operation. The fortress, planted on the summit
of a high rock hard enough to defy the sap and the mine,
was defended by a gallant nobility, supported by the
citizens and a small garrison. After having taken
measures to attack the principal bastion, La Force caused
the regiment commanded by his son to advance to the
assault, but it was so hardly treated as to be obliged to
retire within the lines. Next day Turenne was ordered
with his regiment against the same bastion. All eyes
were fixed on the young colonel. The difficulties were
great ; the besieged, relying not alone on a heavy fire

bore to their ramparts stones of enormous size, which
they launched from the top of the parapet. These, falling
on points of rock, burst into splinters, which, flying in
all directions, killed or maimed the men of the attack.
Turenne, notwithstanding, coolly marched towards the
breach, and his soldiers, drawn on by his example, allowed
no danger to stop them. The besieged, encouraged by their
success of the previous day, made every effort to repel
the attack, Turenne giving his orders with calm presence
of mind amid the dead and the wounded, whom guns,
musketry, and stones stretched on the ground around
him; now doing the duty of leader, now of soldier,
everywhere meeting the desperate movements of the
enemy, pushed him from the bastion, established himself
firmly there, and the fall of La Motte soon followed this
gallant feat of arms. The army loudly praised the success
of Turenne. The marshal in his despatches rendered him
every justice, the court congratulated him, and Richelieu
made him *marechal de camp*—a grade equivalent to that
of major-general, although he was only twenty-three years
old, although it would seem that this promotion was
wrung from the ministry only after the exertion of
private interest. For some time after the taking of La
Motte we find him serving in the rank of colonel at
Landau, Heidelberg, Wissembourg, and Spire—for in his
correspondence he mentions the fine state of his regiment
at Landau, its severe losses at Wissembourg, and its taking
part in the siege of Spire in March, 1635.

Up to this time the Swedes and German Protestants
had only received assistance from France in the form of
diplomacy and subsidies. That kingdom was neither
sufficiently strong nor sufficiently tranquil to undertake
great operations. Gustavus Adolphus, also jealous of

retaining for himself all the results of his expedition,
had shown no desire to associate the French army in his
labours and his dangers. The rapid victories of the
Swedish king had even caused alarm to Richelieu, who
had shown no hurry to fulfil even the engagements which
he had made. But the death of Gustavus at Lutzen in
1632 changed the face of affairs. Bernard of Saxe Weimar
was completely defeated at Nordlingen by the imperial
generals Gallas and Piccolomini. The Elector of Saxony,
in the name of the Lutherans, made his peace with the
emperor at Prague. Banner, who had the command of
the Swedish army on the death of Gustavus, was obliged
to retire on Pomerania, and soon the Swedes had in
Germany no allies of any importance. Then Richelieu
entered resolutely into the contest, and in 1635 displayed
enormous diplomatic activity. He wished not only to
reduce Austria, but, at the same time, Spain. Spanish
soldiers, Spanish treasure, and Spanish generals made in
great part the strength of the imperial armies, and Spain
besides never ceased to ferment internal troubles in
France.

Richelieu signed the treaty of Compiegne with the
Swedes against Ferdinand II. By its conditions he granted
them considerable subsidies in order that they should continue the war in Germany. He made the treaty of St.
Germain en Laye with Bernard of Saxe Weimar, to whom
he promised an annual allowance of money as well as
Alsace, provided that he he should remain in arms to
wrest Franche-Comté from Philip IV. He made the
treaty of Paris with the Dutch, who were to help the
King of France to conquer Flanders, which was to be
divided between France and the United Provinces. He
made the treaty of Rivoli with the dukes of Savoy, of Parma,

and of Mantua, who were to undertake in concert with
France the invasion of the territories of Milan and to
receive a portion of the spoils of Spain. At the same time
he declared war against the Spanish Government, which
had arrested and imprisoned the Elector of Trèves, the
ally of France, and refused to surrender him when demanded. Hostilities immediately began on five different
theatres of war—in the Low Countries, on the Rhine, in
Eastern Germany, in Italy, and in Spain. The army of
the Rhine, commanded by Cardinal de la Valette, was to
operate in conjunction with the corps of Bernard of Saxe
Weimar against the Imperialists, commanded by Count
Gallas. To this army Turenne was attached. It consisted
of 20,000 infantry, 5,000 cavalry, and 14 guns. This was
the army upon which Richelieu mainly relied. The staff
was carefully selected. Besides Turenne we find upon it
the Count of Guiche and the Scotch Colonel Hepburn, as
marshals of camp, Vignolles as sergeant of battle, Fabert,
de la Vigerie, and de l'Échelle as aides-de-camp.

Valette was to annoy the enemy without exposing himself, and was not to approach the Rhine ; but induced by
Bernard, who had a dashing spirit and wished to reconquer
all he had lost, encouraged by the terror of the Imperialists
who raised the siege of Mayence, he determined to pass the
river. He was not long in repenting of that step. He
established his troops round Mayence and revictualled this
place, which was occupied by a Swedish garrison, throwing
in all the supplies of which the town had need. The Imperialists, who had calculated on this imprudence, immediately took to cutting off his supplies, so that soon
everything was wanting in the French camp. Frankfort-
on-Maine made peace with the emperor and abandoned
the Swedish cause. The landgraf of Hesse Cassel, on

whose assistance de la Valette reckoned, promised only his neutrality. Suabia and Franconia showed themselves very doubtful. The scourge of famine threatened the French : it was necessary to retreat, to recross the Rhine, to pass the Sarre, and seek a refuge at Metz. Few retreats have been so difficult and so sad. The army was in such a pitiable condition that round Mayence the men had to be fed with roots and green grapes, and the horses with branches of trees.

When the retreat began the pestilence that stalks in the train of famine in the shape of dysentery, decimated the ranks. It was necessary at once to struggle against the sickness inseparable from scarcity of food and against the enemy, who had supplies in abundance, and bitterly pursued the retreating columns over the woods and rocks of a wasted country. The sick and the weary were abandoned, the guns were buried, villages were burnt to stay the pursuit of the enemy, and to prevent the wretched soldiers who would fall out of the ranks from taking refuge in them. Combats had to be fought to allow time for the retreat. Turenne distinguished himself in those fourteen days of misery and peril in the Palatinate by his devotion to the most wretched of the soldiers, as well as by his gallantry in several engagements. He divided with the men the few provisions that he could find, and threw from his waggons his own baggage to mount upon them soldiers who could no longer march. It is said that finding a soldier dying of hunger and fatigue at the foot of a tree despairing of escape and resolved to abandon his life to the enemy, the general gave him his own horse and marched on foot until he could find a waggon on which to place the sufferer. He consoled some, encouraged others, helped and assisted all without distinction, whether they were or were not of

his own regiment. The enemy endeavoured to get in front
of the retiring columns to cut off their retreat. Turenne
was in command of the advanced guard. He occupied
heights, seized defiles and villages where he could post
infantry, whose fire stopped the Imperialists. At Meizen-
heim he fell upon 4,000 horsemen who barred his passage,
overthrew them, and took their guns from them. His
activity, his courage, and his humanity gained him the
admiration of the army and the gratitude of the court.

When the troops of La Valette had been reorganized at
Pont-a-Moncon, under the active impulsion of Richelieu,
they again took the field against the Imperialists. La
Valette's objective point was Saverne ; the siege of which
he undertook, assisted by the Swedes. Three assaults
were repelled with great loss to the assailants, a fourth
carried one fort, but the town itself was not taken.

Turenne put himself at the head of the French attack,
carried the palisade, passed the ditch, seized the rampart,
and established himself in the place. But he was wounded
by a musket-ball in the right arm, so severely that several
surgeons considered amputation necessary. The operation
was not required, but the alarm with which the rumour of
his danger spread in the army and the joy which his
recovery caused showed what confidence the troops had in
the young general, and the sympathy with which he knew
how to inspire them.

After the capture of Saverne the French and Swedish
armies were directed upon Franche-Comté. This province,
although subject to the King of Spain, was, by the terms
of a treaty with France, to remain neutral. But levies of
troops made there by the Spaniards gave the Cardinal the
pretext for a breach of the neutrality. The great Condé,
Governor of Burgundy, besieged Dôle, Gallas crossing the

Rhine advanced to raise the siege. Turenne was directed
with some troops against Gallas. He fell upon the
Imperialists at Jussey, defeated them, and forced them to
retire with the loss of many prisoners. He then covered
the siege. of Jonville, which the Duke of Weimar undertook, and which soon fell.

In the following year (1637) Turenne distinguished himself in the campaign in Flanders. The Dutch had promised
to make a diversion in this direction against the Spaniards,
and the French Government wished to invade the low
countries both from the side of Picardy with an army
commanded by La Valette, and from Champagne with an
army under Chatillon. La Valette begged that Turenne
should be attached to his staff. After some hesitation it
was determined to enter the province of Hainaut. Some
success marked the opening of the operations. Several
castles were taken, and finally Landrecies was besieged on
the 19th June. Trenches were opened on the 10th July,
and on the 26th the place capitulated.

La Valette then marched further into Belgium, passed
down the Sambre, and sent parties to ravage the country
as far as the gates of Mons, whilst he himself turned
upon Maubeuge. He then took La Capelle, but being
attacked suddenly by the Cardinal Infant, only rescued
his army from a critical position by the presence of mind
and rapid movements of Turenne. The campaign closed,
as was usual in those days, indecisively, for armies were
greatly composed of mercenary troops, and soldiers of
fortune had little zeal to end a war when its conclusion
would terminate the engagment on which they depended
for their livelihood. The more that armies become the
armed population of nations, the shorter will wars be. If
the British army were levied by conscription, and did not

consist of paid volunteers, we might have fewer of the
little wars which are among us so popular, since they
provide excitement for the multitude, and an active circu-
lation for our newspapers.

In the following year (1638), operations were begun
brilliantly by the Duke of Weimar, who, with money
supplied from France, enrolled a corps of 8,000 veteran
Germans. His object was to seize Waldshut and other
towns which lay around Lake Constance. At Rheinfelden
he was checked, but on the 3rd of March he revenged
himself on the enemy, from whom he took their cannon,
their ensigns, their baggage, and four general officers.
Among these was Jean de Werth, who was carried prisoner
to Paris, to the great joy of the Parisians, whom he had
terrified in a previous campaign. Reinforcements were
sent to Weimar from France, and he made himself master
of Rheinfelden on the 23rd of March. He occupied
Freibourg, and undertook the siege of Brisach, which was
the key of Suabia and of southern Germany, and which
he wished to make the capital of a principality for himself. Ferdinand III. sent an army under Goetz to relieve
the place, with orders to save it at all costs. Weimar
asked for further reinforcements from France, which were
sent to him under the command of Turenne and Longueville. Three combats took place, and the Austrians were
driven off without being able to raise the siege. Brisach,
after an assault directed by Turenne, capitulated on the
17th December. By the capture of Brisach, Bernard
conquered all Alsace, occupied the rampart of Germany,
furnished an arsenal for France, gained a defence for
Burgundy, and threw a rein over Austria. Richelieu was
transported with joy. "Courage," said he to Father
Joseph: "Courage, Brisach belongs to us." He was

wrong. Brisach was indeed lost to Austria, but was not yet the property of France, although it had been taken with the aid of the subsidies of France. Bernard would not hear of yielding it, and entrusted it to the keeping of one of his officers, Major-General d'Erlach. Death did not allow the duke to realize his ambition, for he died of fever on the 18th July, 1639, in the thirty-sixth year of his age. Richelieu, for whom this premature death was most fortunate, hastened to buy Weimar's lieutenants, displayed the lilies of France on the towns of Alsace, and entrusted Guébriant to defend the Upper Rhine, which then became the French frontier. Turenne returned to the court, whence the cardinal, having overwhelmed him with praise, sent him to the army of Italy.

Victor Amadeus, Duke of Savoy, who had married Maria Christine, sister of Lewis XIII., had declared for France at the beginning of the rupture with Spain. He died faithful to his alliance on the 7th October, 1637. His duchess soon found herself in a difficult situation. The Spaniards had taken from her Vercelli. The emperor bestowed the regency of the duchy on the Cardinal of Savoy, and on Prince Thomas, brother-in-law of the queen. These, supported by the Duke of Modena and Leganez, Governor of Milan, had published a manifesto to announce that they wished to protect the people against the French, and deliver the young duke, Charles Emmanuel II., the successor of Victor, from French domination.

In the spring of 1639 Prince Thomas entered Piedmont with a Spanish army. Marie Christine implored aid from France, and Cardinal La Valette received orders to support her. His first measures were unfortunate. Fabert and Turenne were sent to his assistance, and soon changed the

aspect of affairs. Turenne aided powerfully in driving back
Leganez and Prince Thomas from Turin, in seizing Chivasso
and in organizing a decisive success, in preparing for
Richelieu two memoirs on the state and the needs of the
army of Italy, and on the direction which should be given
to the war beyond the Alps. Turenne, with his apt spirit
for military organization, proposed the formation of a
regiment of dragoons, and of a company of dragoons to
be attached to each regiment of cavalry. Under Count
d'Harcourt he took part in three considerable affairs. He
commanded on the *Santana,* in the action called that of the
Route of Quiers. He was present at the siege of Turin
and at the taking of Trino.

In accordance with the plan proposed by Fabert to
Richelieu, d'Harcourt had taken Chieri (Quiers), and
revictualled Casale, but through want of provisions was
forced to retreat on Carignano. The Spaniards under
Leganez threw themselves on his rear-guard at the same
time as his advanced guard was attacked by Prince
Thomas, who made a sortie from Turin. Disorder ensued,
but Turenne marched immediately to the front. Fabert
threw four battalions of infantry, into a hollow road whose
fire stopped the enemy's advance. Turenne deployed his
squadrons behind the infantry and launched them unex-
pectedly on the enemy through the intervals of the
battalions. Prince Thomas and the Spaniards were hand-
somely beaten, and on the 20th November, 1639, the
victorious army was safe at Carignano.

D'Harcourt after this campaign took up his winter
quarters at Pinerolo and handed over the command of the
army to Turenne, with instructions to revictual the citadel
of Turin, which was defended by French troops against
Prince Thomas, who had gained most of the town.

Turenne succeeded, notwithstanding the efforts of the besieger, in conveying food and munitions into the citadel.

In the following spring d'Harcourt undertook to relieve Casale, which belonged to the Duke of Mantua, an ally of the French. The place was besieged by Leganez. The command of the cavalry was given to Turenne. The infantry, in three divisions, was led against the entrenchments of the enemy. A skilful movement of Turenne enabled the whole of the troops to be placed in action at once, and the consequence was that d'Harcourt succeeded with 10,000 men in defeating an army larger than his own and strongly entrenched.

After the relief of Casale d'Harcourt resolved, on the advice of Turenne, to besiege Turin. The investment was made on the 10th May, 1640. This siege offered a curious spectacle ; the citadel which the French held was besieged by Prince Thomas, who held the town. He himself was besieged by the French army, which in its turn was besieged in its lines of circumvallation by the Spanish army of Leganez. The place capitulated on the 17th September. Many gallant feats of arms were done during the five months' blockade, and Turenne proved worthy of his reputation for bravery. After he had been wounded by a musket-ball in the shoulder and conveyed to hospital at Pinerolo, so soon as he was cured he returned to the army, bringing with him a strong convoy of food and ammunition. Prince Thomas surrendered ; Leganez recrossed the Po ; Marie Christine re-entered Turin ; and d'Harcourt, being recalled to France by the cardinal, left the command of the army to Turenne.

From this time until he became a Marshal of France his life was divided between military operations and bitter

cares, which the desertion of his brother from the royal
cause gave him.

At the end of the campaign of 1641 Turenne was recalled from the army of Italy, and sent to join that of
Spain.

On the Spanish frontier of France war had been going
on since 1635. There had been continual contests in
Gascony, Languedoc, and Roussillon. In 1640 a revolution
had freed Portugal from the Spanish yoke, and given the
throne to John IV. of the house of Braganza. At the same
time the French fleet had supported a rising in the provinces of Catalonia and Roussillon, which had been fiercely
opposed by the ministers of Philip IV. Richelieu had
allied himself with John IV., had his promised protection
to the Catalans, and in 1642 the French army passed into
Spain and gained the victory of Lerida, while Lewis XIII.
invested Perpignan. Meilleraye commanded the French
troops, and Turenne was named his lieutenant (1642).
Perpignan, Salzces, and four other towns were reduced,
and the conquest of Roussillon was completed in one
campaign.

It was during the siege of Perpignan that Turenne
heard of the treason of his brother, of the ruin of his
house, and of the intention which the cardinal had of
conferring on Fabert the government of Sedan. Turenne
had often cautioned his brother against making an enemy
of the cardinal, but the duke had not listened to his wiser
views. Bouillon had taken part in the conspiracy of the
Count de Soissons in 1641, and had obtained his pardon on
favourable conditions, especially the preservation of all his
privileges and the independence of Sedan. He proved his
gratitude the following year by entering into a conspiracy
with Gaston d'Orleans, and entered into negotiations with

D

Spain, a country at that time engaged in war with his native land. By the terms of this secret treaty the King of Spain was to furnish money and soldiers. The end avowedly aimed at was to make a just peace between the two countries of France and Spain for their common good and that of Christianity.

Richelieu obtained a copy of the treaty. The Duke of Bouillon was clearly implicated; he had just been entrusted with the command of the army of Italy, but on the discovery of the plot was arrested at Casale and imprisoned at Pinerolo. Some of his accomplices were beheaded at Lyons; the brother of the king earned his pardon by cowardice; the Duke of Bouillon only saved his neck at the cost of his principality.

This conspiracy was the last formed against Richelieu. The cardinal died soon afterwards, on the 4th December, 1642, confident on his death-bed when the viaticum was brought to him that his Judge would not condemn him, since in his ministry he had never suggested any cause except for the good of religion and the state. Richelieu had reduced Rochelle, broken down the Huguenot party, joined Lorraine to the French crown, and reduced the greater portion of Alsace.

Lewis XIII. himself died on the 14th May in the following year. His character was feeble, his heart ungenerous; but he knew how to sacrifice his pride to his duty, and he had the virtue, rare among mediocre men, of resigning himself to the guidance of genius. Thanks to this, the house of Bourbon had taken a high position in the world; the domination of Spain in Europe had ended, that of France was about to begin.

CHAPTER III.

Lewis XIII. had never loved Richelieu, but latterly had understood him, and had attached himself to the pursuit of his policy. The king, in dying, left Mazarin prime minister, with all authority necessary to sustain the work of Richelieu. Mazarin adhered to the policy begun by his predecessor for reducing the house of Austria. Many difficulties lay in his way. His enemies were not all outside France. Within there were jealousies, intrigues, civil wars, massacres, frondeurs, conspiracies of the great, revolts of the people. Notwithstanding this, Mazarin continued the war begun by Richelieu, and carried on the contest with the two branches of the house of Austria in Spain, in Italy, in Germany, in Flanders. Great soldiers, French and Swedish, on the one side—Condé, Turenne, Torstenson, Wrangel ; fought against rivals worthy of them on the other—Mercy, Fuentes, and Gallas. Until the peace of Westphalia, Turenne served the court with zeal and ability above all praise, yet he did not enjoy the whole of the confidence of Mazarin, probably on account of his being a Protestant, since it is difficult to find other reasons for the opinion expressed of him in the secret correspondence of the

cardinal. This shows that the statesman had formed an
unfavourable opinion of the soldier, certainly in the year
that he was striving to deprive the Protestants of their
chiefs, the year in which he sought to make the Marshals
de Chatillon and Gassion embrace the Catholic religion, and
when he decided Rantzan to become a Catholic. Turenne
was not of a character to change his religion to please a
minister, nor was he one who would complain of diffidence
shown towards him, nor was he inclined at this time to
unite himself with the malcontents. He was entirely
devoted to his career, to the art of war, to military glory,
and whether he had cause of discontent or not is not
apparent, for he made no recriminations against any one.
Certainly Turenne had no cause of satisfaction with the
conduct of Mazarin towards his brother, the Duke of
Bouillon. This prince had been promised compensation
for the loss of his principality, and Mazarin, who had been
entrusted with the conclusion of the affair, and with
taking possession of the town of Sedan in the name of
the king, was so tardy in giving the prince satisfaction
that it took ten years to settle the question. Turenne
exerted himself in his brother's cause, although still devoted to the court. He might have been happier if he
had always continued under this influence. Mazarin might
have been happier if he had not at last forced Turenne
into opposition. If military conduct could make Mazarin
alter his views, he certainly had good reason to do so in
the year 1643. Turenne was then sent into Italy to command an independent corps, but was instructed to take
orders from Prince Thomas of Savoy, who had abandoned
the Spanish party and allied himself with France. The
prince, however, was looked on doubtfully by the French
Government, and while given the commission of general

of the armies of the king, it was considered desirable to attach to him a man of proved fidelity. The choice fell on Turenne. As soon as he arrived in the valley of the Po, the two generals made a demonstration against Alexandria in order to lead the Spaniards to withdraw their garrison from Trino, a strong fortress of Piedmont on the Po, which they wished to reduce. The stratagem succeeded. The Spaniards passed into Alexandria a large portion of the provisions and garrisons of Trino. This was what Turenne expected. He quickly broke up from Alexandria and blockaded and attacked Trino; it was reduced at the end of six weeks.

Whilst still before this town Turenne received orders to return to France. The Regency had not yet come to terms with the house of Bouillon, and it was feared that the discontent which the Protestant party manifested on this account might shake the fidelity of Turenne. The minister considered it wise to satisfy the legitimate ambition of the young lieutenant-general, to recompense his brilliant services, and to strengthen his loyalty. While his brother was promised that new advantages should be given in exchange for the principality of Sedan, to Turenne himself was granted the proud distinction of a baton of Marshal of France. He was then thirty-two years of age. He had been four years a captain, four years a colonel, three years major-general, five years lieutenant-general. He had served under four general officers. These were the Prince of Orange, his uncle, to whom he said that he owed the knowledge of how to choose well a camp and attack well a fortress; the Duke of Weimar, who he said gained mighty results with no resources; Cardinal La Valette, from whom he had learned to discard the delicacy and gallantry of the court and assume a military tone; and Count d'Harcourt, from whom he learned that diligence and energy are the main means of success in warlike affairs. Circumstances soon showed that he was worthy to exercise a high and independent charge.

After the death of Bernard of Saxe Weimar, Marshal Guébriant had been placed in command of the troops of Weimar. He had besieged and taken Rottweil in Suabia, but had there been killed. Rantzan, who succeeded him in command of the Weimar army, marched (24—25 Nov., 1643) upon Dütlingen, on the Upper Rhine, was there beaten by Mercy and made prisoner, with the loss of many officers and 7,000 soldiers. This was a great triumph for the Bavarians ; a terrible disaster for France. The whole of the German infantry in the French service was dispersed or taken, the cavalry retreated as they best could upon the Rhine. Mazarin showed much foresight and much firmness in this danger. Turenne had only been received at court on the 16th November as Marshal. He as yet had no command. Mazarin, laying aside his doubts in the cause to the advantage of the state, chose him to command on the frontier of the Rhine, and charged him with the duty of re-establishing the army of Weimar. Sacrificing the interests of his family to those of his country, Turenne accepted the mission. He knew Germany ; he was known by the soldiery of Weimar. He had the calmness, the clearness, the tenacity of Guébriant. It was certain that he would be well received by the troops, and would quickly re-establish the situation beyond the Rhine. Circumstances required active measures. Plenipotentiaries had just assembled at Münster to begin the negotiations which ended with the peace of Westphalia. It was desired that the French Government should support the French diplomatist by quick successes. The

French allies were doubtful; it was necessary to re-
assure them. The enemies of France were already beginning to forget the brilliant victory of Rocroi, which had
been won in the early summer, and looked upon the
disaster at Dütlingen as not only an irreparable catastrophe, but as the destruction of the French army.
Mazarin skilfully took all measures necessary. Turenne
was sent to the Rhine with reinforcements of cavalry and
infantry, and with money in abundance to purchase provisions and stores and other necessaries. Levies of men
were made. It was necessary, in placing Turenne in command of this army, to pass over d'Erlach, who was then
Governor of Freibourg. This general was so hurt that he
resolved to quit the service of France, but Turenne, with
tact and delicacy, soothed his ruffled feelings, and persuaded him to remain as Governor of Brisach. This little
coolness having been removed, d'Erlach continued to
France his good and loyal service, and Turenne employed
the winter of 1643–4 in reorganizing his army. He
made great sacrifices and borrowed considerable sums to
place it on a proper footing. He re-established discipline,
and breathed into it a new spirit. He hurried through
Alsace, which had been devastated by war, put its towns
into a state of defence, established his cantonments behind
the Vosges, in Lorraine, and in Franche-Comté. To give
them wider scope he took Luxeiul and Vesoul from the
Spaniards. At the same time, by negotiations, the
prisoners who had been taken at Dütlingen were restored
to France, the gaps in the ranks were filled up, and in
the spring of 1644 Turenne found himself at the head of
9,000 men, of whom 5,000 were cavalry, and was in a
position to take the field.

CHAPTER IV.

TURENNE had now gained a military position and an influence in the state which allowed his individual character to be felt in the organization and administration of armies, in the strategy of campaigns, and in the tactics of battles.

The theatres of war on which he fought were widely different in their physical aspects from those on which a general may be expected to manœuvre in our days.

In the seventeenth century, agriculture, which has now been raised to the dignity of a science, was hardly understood, even in its primary rudiments. A few fields only were tilled in the immediate neighbourhood of towns or hamlets, and were sown every year with continuous crops until the ground, rendered barren through exhaustion, refused to yield any further produce. This patch of land was then left for many years fallow to regain its fecundity by the wholesome, though tedious, operations of nature. Drainage was almost unknown. The long lines of chaussées edged with stately poplars, which now lead from town to town and from village to village, throughout the continent of Europe, were unknown. It was not until the later

years of Lewis XIV. that these were constructed, even
to a distance of fifty miles from Paris. Roads, at the
beginning of that reign, were mere tracks with undrained
bottoms, on which stones were thrown, in order to afford
some sort of foothold. These quickly sinking deep into
the moist soil, were replaced by slush and mire, which, in
wet weather, became little more easy to travel over than a
quicksand. Bridges were few, and only found at the
principal passages over great rivers. Roads usually
crossed streams by fords, to which they painfully led
through bogs, morasses, and quagmires. The skill of the
civil engineer consisted merely in occasionally avoiding
formidable heights. As a general rule, the roads led
directly across natural obstacles, for levelling and survey-
ing were unheeded. In such a low state was agriculture
that there were no means of keeping animals for food alive
during winter. The whole of the small quantity of hay or
dry grass which could be collected in summer-time was
required in winter to sustain with difficulty the animals
which were necessary in the coming spring to stock the
flocks, to provide beasts of burden for carriage, or beasts
of haulage for the plough.

During the reign of Lewis XIV., after the death of
Mazarin, and after the king himself seized the reins of
government, great improvements were made in France.
But when Richelieu died the Italians still described all the
nations which lived beyond the Alps as barbarians, and
it must be owned that these in great measure deserved the
title.

The French probably less than other nations enjoyed
those arts which cultivate luxury, and of which the absence
is an almost certain proof that arts which provide necessities were neglected or unknown. If what is necessary is

brought to perfection, the beautiful and agreeable follow.
It is not surprising that painting, sculpture, poetry, elo-
quence, philosophy, were almost totally absent from a
nation, which, although it possessed ports on the Atlantic,
in the Channel, and on the Mediterranean, still had no
fleet, and which, although inclined to idolise luxury, had at
that time few factories even of coarse goods.

The Genoese, the Venetians, the Portuguese, the Flemish,
the Dutch, and the English, turn by turn carried on the
commerce of France while she was ignorant even of commercial principles.

Lewis XIII. at his accession had not a vessel.   Paris
did not, in the time of Richelieu, contain 400,000 men, and
did not possess four fine buildings.   The other towns of the
kingdom were mere hamlets.   The nobility lived in the
country, in keeps surrounded with ditches, and oppressed
the cultivators of the soil.   The roads were almost impracticable, the towns were without police, the State without
money, the Government almost always without credit.

Lewis XI. had done much to raise the royal power, but
nothing for the happiness of the nation.   Francis I. endeavoured to raise commerce, navigation, letters, and the arts,
but he was unable to make them take root in his country,
and they died with him.   Henry the Great might have
restored to France the security and happiness which thirty
years of civil discord had expelled, when he was assassinated in the midst of the people whose happiness he
wished to achieve.

Richelieu engaged in the reduction of the house of
Austria, struggling with Calvinism and with the great
nobles, had not time for peaceful reforms.   Thus, in the
early part of the seventeenth century, the nobility were
uncurbed, uncontrolled, and ignorant of everything, except

wars, duels, selfishness, and sloth. The clergy, living in disorder and ignorance, traded on the superstitions of the vulgar. The people, without industries or manufactories, grovelled in wretchedness.

The French took no part in the grand discoveries nor splendid inventions of other nations. Printing, gunpowder, looking-glasses, telescopes, the compass, the air-pump, the true system of the universe, had never been investigated in France. The French nobility still disported themselves in tournaments, while the Portuguese and Spaniards were discovering and conquering new worlds in the East and West. Charles V. was already lavishing in Europe the treasures of Mexico before some subjects of Francis I. had discovered the bleak uplands that lie along the St. Lawrence.

In the great affairs of Europe France was of little importance. Supremacy over the civilized world swayed between the branch of the Imperial house that reigned at Madrid and the other branch that ruled at Vienna. Since the abdication of Charles V., notwithstanding the defeat of Philip's Armada, and through the splendid reputation which the famed infantry of Spain had won upon the field of St. Quentin, and which by its prestige for nearly 100 years awed foreigners from insulting the Spanish nation, the whole of our continent looked with awe, reverence, and respect upon the house of Austria. The family of Charles V. was predominant in Europe. This house, in the first half of the seventeenth century, although struck with a palsy which was not apparent to the world in general, still was mistress of Spain, Portugal, and the treasures of America, the Low Countries, the districts of Milan, the kingdoms of Naples, Bohemia, Hungary, and had enormous influence in Germany. If the descendants of Charles V. had possessed his vigour—if, indeed, on his abdication his power had not been divided—Europe might have been subjected to Spain, and been drawn down in the gradual decline of a country which has indeed never fallen, but since his time has ever decayed.

The state of a country has a large influence on its military force, and in the early half of the seventeenth century the military force of France was very poor. A portion consisted of mercenary troops hired from Germany. Turenne himself was probably the greatest of the military reformers who urged upon the councils of the king the necessity of reorganization, of raising the condition of the soldier, and of instituting short service. But it was not for many years that his views were adopted, or his advice followed. At the time at which we have arrived, France had probably at the most 80,000 effective men scattered on the five theatres of war on which she was then engaged. The soldiery were enlisted for life, but were allowed at the termination of every campaign to leave the company in which they were enrolled, and to join the company of any other captain whom they preferred. Thus the men had no respect for the traditions of their regiments, or for fidelity to their comrades or commanders. Commerce, which has so extensively spread in our days, was then in the hands of the few. The police was entirely neglected, a certain proof of a wretched administration.

Richelieu had, indeed, begun to make France formidable without, but could do nothing to make her flourishing within. The roads were neither repaired nor guarded, and were infested with brigands; the streets of Paris, narrow, badly paved, and covered with disgusting filth, were filled with thieves. Voltaire tells that the registers of the Parliament show that the watch of the capital was

reduced to forty-five men, so ill paid that they never turned
out for duty.

Since the death of Francis II., France had been continually troubled with civil wars or internàl factions; the yoke
of the Crown had never been borne peacefully or cheerfully.
The nobility had been nurtured in the foul atmosphere of
conspiracy and faction. These were the means by which
power, rank, and title were achieved, as afterwards were
flattery to the monarch or attentions to his mistress. The
spirit of discord and faction had from the capital. penetrated
even into the smallest towns. Men everywhere disputed
and quarrelled, and sought their remedies in brute force
because the State was powerless and the law impotent. The
very parishes of Paris had combats between themselves,
and sacred processions fought for the honour of their re-
spective banners. The canons of Notre Dame often were
engaged in fisticuffs with the canons of St. Chapelle. Parliament itself and the Court of Exchequer fought with
cudgels for the front place in the cathedral of Notre Dame
on the day that Lewis XIII. placed his kingdom under the
protection of the Virgin (15th August, 1638).

Every one bore arms, and drew them freely in the cause
of their city, their guild, or themselves. Duels were constant. This barbarism, authorised in ancient times by the
kings themselves, contributed as much as civil and foreign
wars to depopulate the country. It is estimated that in
the course of twenty years, ten of which had been troubled
with foreign war, more French gentlemen died by the
hands of Frenchmen than by those of their enemies.

The nation was plunged in ignorance, which extended to
the highest classes. Astrologers were consulted and believed in. All the memoirs of that time are full of pre-
dictions. Even the grave and severe Sully solemnly

recounts those that were made to Henry IV. This credulity, an infallible token of ignorance, was so widely spread that an astrologer was carefully kept hidden in the room of Anne of Austria at the moment of the birth of Lewis XIII. Witchcraft and the possession of devils was thoroughly believed in and regarded as a sacred truth. Priests made a special profession of exorcising demons. The courts of law, which should be more enlightened than the vulgar, frequently were occupied in judging sorcerers, and it will ever be a stain on the memory of Richelieu that he allowed the judicial murder of the famous Curé de Loudun, Urbain Grandier, who was sentenced to be burnt at the stake as a magician.

An account of one of the trials in connection with sorcery shows how little the horse was understood or esteemed in those days, and how miserable and wretched must have been the animals on which cavalry were mounted. A charge was laid against a horse-dealer that he had allowed his horse to be cleaned, and so terrible was the crime considered that there was a strong attempt made to have both the horse and its master burnt at the stake.

The Calvinist party, to which many of the nobility belonged, and with which some of the superior clergy had sympathy, looked on the Catholic religion as idolatry, and hated it with a stern and fierce abhorrence because of their firm conviction that the Church, not content with enforcing idolatry on its own congregations, thirsted to spread its idolatries and uncompromising tenets by fire and sword throughout the land at large. The Calvinists, themselves not altogether free from popular superstitions, marked their severance from the Church by the harsh manners and severe countenances that are so often characteristic of reformers. The geniality, the lightness of heart, the wit,

and the merriment which now distinguish the French
nation were then absolutely unknown. There were no
houses where society met together to communicate views
or exchange ideas. The Academy, which was founded in
1635, had hardly made any perceptible influence. There
were no amusements; everything for which we consider life
worth living was ignored for the grovelling need of main-
taining life itself. Theatres, customs, laws, arts, society,
religion, peace and war, were totally different from what
they became in the later glorious reign of Lewis XIV.,
who, supported by a brilliant circle of statesmen and
captains, left France a totally different country from what
he found it when he took over the government from
Mazarin.

In countries impracticable in winter through want of
drainage and absence of communications, it was impossible
to carry on military operations in bad weather. As a rule,
armies broke up in the autumn and separated into winter
quarters. In the summer, too, the operations of war were
very different from those we witness in our days.

Armies were small. A force of 10,000 men, which would
be now looked upon as little more than a brigade, was then
deemed a force worthy to be commanded by a marshal of
France. In countries exposed to brigands, to thieves, and
to the ravages of mercenary soldiers, it was impossible for
the farmer to store with security supplies, or for the
merchant to establish manufactories. The trim homestead,
the well-stocked stack-yards, which are now to be found
near every hamlet, were then unknown; the busy mills
now to be seen on the banks of every rocky stream were
nowhere to be found. Stores, supplies, and all necessaries
of life, except for the very humblest and most miserable
peasantry, were perforce placed for protection within the

ramparts of fortified towns, where the armourer and the weaver followed out their craft slowly and laboriously, unaided by steam or machinery.

Fortified towns were then frequent, and as armies were not of sufficient size to invest them and pass them by, and march straight upon a hostile capital, wars consisted in great measure of sieges. In modern times, when armies are mustered by millions, such garrisons as those which Mons, Brisach, or Ostend contained, some 1,200 or 1,300 men, would merely cause the detachment of a corps to hold them in check, to prevent them from issuing forth and annoying the communications of the invading force, and would not for a day delay the march of the main columns towards the enemy's metropolis.

The spirit of chivalry still existed, and men considered it more noble to fight on horseback than on foot, hence there was a natural inclination for armies to be composed in great part of cavalry. The infantry soldier also was unable, in case of disaster, to seek any refuge. There were no villages to which he might hurry. There were no farm-houses in which to seek repose or refreshment. In the event of a battle lost with a pursuing enemy he must either become a prisoner, when his fate was indeed miserable, and he lost his arms, without which he could gain no employment as a mercenary soldier, and his occupation was gone, or he was trampled down under the hoofs of the pursuing cavalry. The infantry soldier could carry little with him in the way of either food or clothing. His armament was heavy. The roads were toilsome, and there were no magazines, no baggage trains. It was only when the army was established either in intrenchments or engaged upon a siege that convoys were organized to supply the troops with provisions.

But the cavalry itself, although better off than the infantry, was very different from the cavalry which is seen in our day. The whirlwind rush with which a brigade of hussars dashes up the long valley at Aldershot, or a regiment of Life Guards thunders across Windsor Park, were then unknown. The horses were poor and sorry, and were heavily weighted. Even in the fiercest shock of battle, charges were delivered and received at a trot. Cavalry really trusted more to their fire-arms than to their swords. They were usually drawn up in three, four, or even six ranks, and slowly and painfully, in case of fighting on horseback, trotted against each other. Infantry, who were armed chiefly with pikes, and to whom only a few musketeers or matchlock men were attached, had no power of fire with which to keep cavalry at a distance, and frequently the horse-soldiers rode up close to the serried battalion of pikemen, and calmly at their ease picked off the officers with their pistols. The chief use of cavalry, however, except in case of pursuit, was to fight on foot. As a general rule, all the cavalry were what was known afterwards as dragoons, whose horses were only useful as vehicles for bringing them into action, and for carrying them out again when pressed by a superior force.

On the first invention of gunpowder, the tendency of equipment had been to increase the strength and weight of defensive armament. The armour of the knights of the Crusades was found useless against bullets urged upon breastplate or headpiece by the force of the new explosive gas, but it was soon found that the increased weight of armaments, without stopping the bullets, merely prevented horsemen from manœuvring. By the time at which we have arrived, a considerable change had taken place in the

ordinary equipment of the cavalry soldier, which can be
clearly seen from Bourgogne's pictures, who was a contemporary of Turenne. The cuirass and steel headpiece
were still maintained, and the arm was clothed in armour
down to the elbow. On ceremonial occasions it appears
too that the thighs were incased in steel, but usually the
body and head alone were thus protected. The heavy
greaves had been replaced by the jack-boot, and the
gauntlets of steel by long leather gloves.

The majority of the infantry consisted of pikemen
armed with a pike some fourteen feet long, and were
drawn up in heavy battalions of twelve or even fourteen
ranks deep. Attached to each battalion, or placed in the
intervals between them, were parties of musketeers who
were posted in ranks of six or eight deep. The best shots
were often placed in the front rank, and the remaining
ranks closed up to these one by one, and handed them new
weapons ready loaded with which to fire. The artillery,
which was rude and difficult to move, consisted generally
of 4-pounder or 6-pounder guns, which were drawn by
heavy horses or animals that could be found in the country.
Naturally, whenever a reverse occurred, or the army had
to retreat hastily, the owners of the horses or bullocks
employed for the artillery did their best to get away with
their animals, and consequently guns were almost invariably abandoned and lost in case of the slightest disorder.
Yet this is the identical system for transporting artillery
which even nowadays the enlightened spirits of the
Department of the Adjutant-General of Royal Artillery
would wish to introduce for manœuvring the guns that are
expected to defend England against invasion.

Turenne was one of the first to loudly declaim against
such a mode of moving cannon, and to point out the

insecurity and folly of the system. It cannot however be expected that an adjutant-general of the present day should be sufficiently conversant with the French language as to have read the memoirs of Turenne.

Since nearly every town was fortified as soon as an army entered a theatre of war, it was necessary to make sieges. If it left a fortified town behind it, the garrison would have issued and acted on its rear, or cut off its communications. Towns, too, as a rule covered the bridges over rivers, and it was extremely difficult, on account of the absence of artificial drainage, for armies to approach rivers except at bridges. Hence we find that the operations of war, before the time of Turenne, were mainly limited to sieges, and he was one of the first to show how the power of manœuvring was more important indirectly as a strategical operation than were investments or blockades. As he himself said, " It is a great mistake to waste men in taking a town when the same expenditure of soldiery will gain a province." It is an error always to sacrifice life when the same object, or often even a greater, can be achieved by rapidity of movement.

The state of the country led also in part to the constant adoption of intrenchments. Roads were few and far between. If an army took up a position, it was difficult for it to be attacked except along some well-known line of communication. The general was well aware from what point his enemy must appear, and if he could intrench his front, resting his flanks upon some natural obstacles immediately close to him, he was tolerably certain of not being outflanked or obliged to leave his intrenchments in consequence of some brilliant manœuvre of his adversary. The fronts of armies were much smaller in proportion to the number of men in their

ranks than at the present time. We have seen that
cavalry was frequently drawn up in as many as six ranks.
Infantry was constantly formed for battle twelve or fourteen
ranks deep. Thus there was plenty of labour ready among
the soldiery to cover with strong intrenchments and
broad ditches the whole front of the line of battle. At
the present time, when troops fight in extended order, it
would be impossible to intrench an army in the manner
in which intrenchments were understood in the seventeenth century. It is indeed of great advantage that
every soldier should carry with him some implement
with which he can throw up some slight cover, for behind this he or the guns that accompany him may take
shelter and be protected from the rifle bullets of the
enemy. But to intrench an army of the present day in
the mode in which intrenchments were used in the time
of Turenne would be a simple waste of time and labour.
If the intrenchments were stretched along the whole
front of the force, and were really formidable, an enemy
would not come near them, but would choose one of the
many roads by which he could reach his objective point,
and pass widely round their flank. He would thus,
without assailing them, pass them by, perhaps after
amusing their garrison with a false attack, and the intrenchments once turned must be abandoned, and would
fall of themselves. If, on the other hand, the works were
weakly dotted along the front of the army holding them,
they would have but a slight perceptible influence on the
field of battle. In fact, under modern conditions, if a
system of retrenchments were adopted, they would, if
weak, be rushed, if strong, avoided.

A peculiarity of war in the seventeenth century was
that when a force were taken prisoners the men as a rule

were returned to the country under whose banner they were fighting. This was not only a relic of the beneficial influence which the Church had exerted by nobly raising her voice against the system of slavery, but it was also dictated by humanity and by the peculiar circumstances of war at that time. In those days, when armour and armaments were produced slowly, painfully, and without machinery, the strength of fighting hosts lay not so much in numbers and men as in the quality of their equipment. When a force fell prisoners into the enemy's hands, it was extremely difficult to feed them. If they were fed from the resources which the captor himself possessed, they diminished his own means of feeding his own men. If they were left to starve, they would breed disease and infection in his camp. Hence every motive prevailed to restore them to his enemy ; nor was their restoration of great value, for their arms and equipments were taken from them, and in those days it was extremely difficult to find arms or equipment for any considerable force.

The Arsenal at Woolwich or the factories of Essen probably turn out more military armaments in the course of a week than did the sword-makers of Toledo or the armourers of Mons in the course of a century at the time which we are considering.

The actual army of France, such as it was in the days of Turenne, had been the gradual growth of the Guards of the sovereign, which probably existed from the commencement of the monarchy. At the head of all the troops of France, until the time of the Revolution, stood on the muster-roll that far-famed body the Maison de Roi, or the Household Brigade. The grandeur of this corps dates from the time of Francis I., when it was composed of a total force of some 800 men, of whom 200 were gentlemen, some bodyguards, consisting of a Scotch company, Scotch archers, three French companies, and 100 Swiss. This organisation was not sensibly modified until a later period than that of which we are now speaking (1664), but the Scotch company had come to be more and more composed of French, and little was preserved of its origin except the habit of giving the commands in the Scotch tongue.

Henry IV. (1593) had added to the Household Brigade a company of light horse as well as a company of 200 men-at-arms. He also added a company of carbineers. It was this company which in 1622 took the name of the celebrated Musketeers of the King when Lewis XIII. gave them the musket. Richelieu and Mazarin both had guards of musketeers of their own, and the latter made his a present to Lewis XIII. It was only when the reorganisation of the army took place in 1664, under the advice of Turenne, that musketeers were added to each company of the Household Brigade.

The men of whom this corps consisted were the sons of burgesses or farmers, who enrolled themselves in order to escape from taxation and to enjoy an easy and agreeable life. They had to pay the captains for places in the corps. They never went to war except when the sovereign joined the camp, and in no case at this time did they fight. They merely performed the duties of escort and guard.

It was from this militia of ornament and parade that Lewis XIV., aided by Turenne, made the famous cavalry of France, and a nursery of officers for the active army, which became famous in Europe.

The cavalry, as we have seen, had considerable advantages over the infantry. Each horseman carried provisions for a certain time on his horse, and in case of being wounded or ill could be conveyed on horseback to a place of safety. The foot-soldier under the same circumstances, unable to march, had neither hospital nor security. At the battle of Dutlingen we see that the cavalry was able to gain the Rhine and so save itself, but the whole of the infantry was destroyed or taken prisoners. It was in the time of Richelieu that the French cavalry was divided into regiments on the advice of Fabert. This system of organisation had existed for some time in the Spanish and German armies, but hitherto in the French the cavalry had only been divided into squadrons, and when squadrons were placed together a captain commanded all. There was no intermediate grade between the general commanding the whole cavalry and the captain commanding squadrons (1638).

Lewis XIV. also made an important change in the mode by which officers were supplied to the cavalry, for we find that on the 13th April, 1658, he notified to Turenne that orders should be issued to the officers of his troops to the effect that in future no officer should receive a commission in the gendarmerie or cavalry who had not already had experience of two years in the infantry. The gendarmerie was like our Life Guards, the first regiment of cavalry. Until the reign of Francis I. none had been admitted to its ranks except gentlemen who could give proof of nobility. At first all cavalry which was not part of the gendarmerie was light cavalry, and was divided as we have seen into regiments.

In 1635 Lewis XIII. had formed six regiments of light cavalry, which comprised some companies of carbineers. Ten new regiments were made between 1642 and 1656; and during the Dutch wars Lewis XIV. had on foot ninety regiments of cavalry, of which the muster rolls on the 1st of January, 1678, included 47,000 horses. The

principal regiments were distinguished by the title of
Royal, such as the Royal Roussillon, the Royal Piedmont, the Royal German, the Royal Carbineers. The
others were called after the name of their colonels. Thus
the regiment of Turenne, which was raised under the name
of Tiangs in 1666, became Florensac in 1664, Talmont
in 1693, Turenne in 1710, and Gramont in 1735. Some
regiments bore the names of provinces.

Two-thirds of the armies which Turenne first commanded
were composed of horsemen. In the war of Devolution
about half of the army consisted of cavalry. In 1672,
when Lewis XIV. took the field, three-fourths of his force
was formed of infantry, and a new era in the art of war
then began. Infantry was increased in proportion as the
aristocratic arm decreased, and the peasantry began to
enter more and more into the composition of the French
army.

One of the great faults of the French infantry, until
Louvois under the advice of Turenne reorganised it, was
that the soldiers did not remain in the same companies,
but changed their captains at every rumour of a disagreeable garrison or an unpleasant duty. Discipline was impossible, and although the men were all of long service they
were new to their comrades and unknown to their officers.

Turenne demanded, in 1656, that each captain should be
obliged to keep in his company during winter at least
twenty men; that these should be mustered by commissaries, and that the captain should be assured of the
money necessary to support them. The infantry was formed
into battalions in 1635.

The four first regiments of French infantry were the
ancient bands of Francis I. and Henry II., the regiments
of Picardy, Piedmont, Navarre, Champagne. These were

distinguished by the name of Vieux. Others followed
who had been created in the time of Henry IV., and were
called Petits Vieux, of which there were only five remaining. On the accession of Louis XIV., the Rambures,
Silly, Auvergne, Sault and Epagne. These, with the
regiments of Normandy and the marine, and with those of
Saint-Villier, Douglas, the King's Regiment and that of
Lorraine, ranked after the regiments of French Guards
and the regiments of Swiss Guards. They held strongly
to their name and privileges, the most important of which
was not to be disbanded, but merely reduced, after a war ;
and when Lewis XIV. raised the regiment in 1662, of
which he was colonel, and of which Martinet, a name still
known as that of a formidable commanding officer, was
lieutenant-colonel, the king did not dare to place it above
these ancient bands. The old regiments were continually
increased. Eighteen were added under Lewis XIII. In
1666 Lewis XIV. had over 47,000 foot, and in 1714 he
had 264 infantry regiments of Frenchmen and foreigners.
Of these 222 had been raised in his own reign. These
mustered 114,500 men. In the foreign corps were Irish,
Scotch, Germans, Italians, Walloons. A regiment consisted of three battalions ; a battalion of twelve or
fifteen companies ; and a company of fifty or sixty men.
At the time of the war in Holland one-third of the
infantry were armed with pikes, and formed the centre of
the battalion ; the other two-thirds were provided with
muskets or arquebusses. The pikemen were armed with
pike and sword, the musketeers with wheel muskets,
which in firing they rested on a forked stock that they
carried with them. Officers who marched in front of
companies, and sergeants who guided on the flanks, were
armed with small pikes or halberds.

In 1667, and in 1669, two important changes were made
in the army. Grenadiers were substituted for the *enfants
perdus.* These were soldiers chosen by lot from the various
companies to march in advance of the columns to lead the
assault, to scout and to skirmish. They disappear in
1658, and were replaced nine years later by grenadiers.
There were originally four men in each company who were
told off to throw grenades. In 1670 Lewis XIV. joined
all the grenadiers of his own regiment together and
formed one company of them. This was the first company
of grenadiers regularly organised. Afterwards one was
formed in each regiment, and they were armed with fire-
arms and bayonets, the wooden butts of which were stuck
into the barrel of the musket and removed for firing. It
was only some twelve years later that the socket for the
bayonet was invented.

In 1669 dragoons were specially formed. Little by little
their value was appreciated, and the number of the regiments was accordingly increased from two to fourteen.

Turenne, as we have seen, was the first to advocate the
formation of dragoons. Before the time of Louvois officers
of artillery and of engineers were distinct from the army,
and had no military rank. They bought their position
from the master-general of the ordnance. Guns were
worked under the direction of these officers by gunners
who were enlisted for the war and discharged when
peace was made. These officers also superintended the
construction of batteries in case of siege, and gained considerable emolument from the difference between the price
paid by the government and the expenses which they were
obliged to bestow on securing gunners and keeping up
their guns. The master-general on his side obtained large
profits from towns which capitulated after having been

bombarded, for, according to the custom of the day, everything of copper or of iron, excepting the artillery, was his
by right, and he had the privilege of selling them if their
proprietors did not arrange with him. In 1668 six companies of gunners were formed, and a special regiment of
fusiliers raised as guards for the artillery. In the same
regiment was a company of sappers and two companies of
military workmen. Thus the artillery took its place in
the army.

Before this time, when a siege had to be undertaken,
officers were selected from the infantry for tracing the
works of the attack. Vauban himself was a captain in the
regiment of Picardy, and when engaged in the superin-
tendence of the works at the siege of Lille in 1667, was
obliged to beg of Louvois the special favour of being excused
from mounting ordinary guards.

The high administration of the army was curiously
complicated. There were four Secretaries of State in
France to divide the administration of affairs, and until
1667 the Secretary for War controlled in his Department
only the fortifications of Artois, Roussillon, and Dau-
phiny, and his other three colleagues superintended the
fortresses which were in the provinces of their Depart-
ments.

Richelieu, notwithstanding this difficulty, considerably
increased the defences of France, especially on the Atlantic
Ocean, and on the Meuse and Moselle.

When armies were concentrated and placed in the field,
the squadrons and battalions were divided into brigades,
but the number of brigades of which an army was composed was always divided into seven parts.

The order of battle consisted of two lines and a reserve.
Each line was composed of a body of infantry in the centre

and a body of cavalry on either wing. The reserve was
formed of troops of the two armies united into one corps.
In modern language, it might be said that there were two
divisions of infantry, four of cavalry, and one mixed
division. Troops had places in the line which their
privileges allowed them to demand. The household
brigades and the gendarmerie were always on the right
wing, the French and the Swiss guards in the centre of the
first line. Battalions and squadrons were parted from one
another by intervals equal to their front. Those of the
second line and the reserve covered the intervals in the
line in front of them. Battalions were drawn up with the
pikemen massed in the centre and musketeers on the
wings. When cavalry charged a battalion, the musketeer
fired while the pikeman remained powerless. If the fire of
the musketry did not stay the charge, the pikemen,
holding the butts of their pikes against the right foot,
took up the defence, while the musketeer remained an idle
but not disinterested spectator of the combat, for if the
pikeman was borne down it was all over both with him
and the musketeer. The artillery were generally in front
of the line, and began the action by cannonading the
enemy ; then the cavalry on the wings charged the cavalry
opposed to it, and if it succeeded, and the horsemen could
be again gathered together, they were brought against the
flank of the infantry, such as was the case at the battles of
Lutzen, Rocroi, and the Dunes. Very often the victorious
cavalry could not be recalled, and lost itself in pillaging
the camp or baggage of the other side.

    The military operations of the seventeenth century are
interesting to historical students, because they show how
great deeds were done by great men under great difficulties. They are, too, of interest, as are the campaigns of

Hannibal, Scipio, or Cæsar, since they show how the broad principles of the science of war are constant in all generations ; but the student who would forecast the future, or would qualify himself for useful service in modern campaigns, must pass over the campaigns of Condé to grasp those of Napoleon, must put aside the strategy of Turenne to dive into that of Moltke.

The principles of the military art have been the same in all ages, but victory has ever smiled upon the strategist who, not content with a blind acceptance of principle, has developed details and worked out the niceties of time, distance, and topography with the accuracy of a mathematician and the patient skill of an astronomer.

CHAPTER V.

RICHELIEU and Lewis XIII. were dead, the one admired
and hated, the other quickly forgotten. They had bequeathed to the French nation an aversion for the very
name of minister, and little respect for the throne. Lewis,
by his will, established a Council of Regency. The first act
of his widow, Ann of Austria, was to cause the will of her
husband to be declared null and void by a decree of the
Parliament of Paris. This body, long opposed to the court,
quashed the will of the king as calmly as it would have
settled the cause of a private citizen. By the same decree,
Gaston, Duke of Orleans, uncle of the king, received the
empty title of Lieutenant-General of the Kingdom under an
absolute Regency.

Ann of Austria was forced to continue the war against
Philip IV. of Spain, her brother. Some months before
Turenne took up the command on the upper Rhine, the
Spanish government, confident in the weakness of a
minority, and seeing the army opposite to their frontier in
the Low Countries commanded by a young man of twenty-
one years old, sent across the frontiers of Hainaut
26,000 men under the experienced General Niello. Cham-

pagne was harried, Rocroi was besieged, and the Spaniards
thought they would send their scouts to the very gates of
Paris ; but the young man who stood opposite to them
with an inferior army was Lewis de Bourbon, Duke of
Enghien, known afterwards as the great Condé. Most
successful generals have become so by degrees. This prince
was a born leader of armies. The art of war seemed in
him a natural instinct. He and Torstenson are the only
men of the seventeenth century who, at twenty years of
age, had that genius which surpasses experience. Condé
had received with the news of the death of Lewis XIII. an
order not to risk a battle. The marshal who was given to
him as a counsellor supported this timid policy. The prince
(19th May, 1643) obeyed neither court nor counsellor. He
forced on a battle. Near Rocroi he attacked with his
cavalry the cavalry opposed to him, drove it off the field,
and wheeled round upon the flank of the Spanish infantry,
till then regarded in Europe as invincible. Their battalions
stood as firm in their dark and serried ranks as the ancient
phalanx. Their files opened with a mobility that the
phalanx never possessed, to allow the discharge against
Condé's horsemen of eighteen guns concealed in their
centre. Nevertheless, the prince, with his mounted men-
at-arms, surrounded the dreaded pikemen and arquebusiers
of Spain. Twice he madly charged them : twice his
squadrons were hurled back in disorder. A third attack
was crowned with success. The horsemen dashed through
the musketry fire, bore down the pikes and halberds levelled
against them, and scattered in headlong rush the most
renowned infantry in the world. The Spanish officers
threw themselves at the feet of Condé for quarter, while
the grand old general, Fuentes, who commanded them, died
on the field pierced with wounds. Condé, on learning his

death, exclaimed "that he should have wished to die like
Fuentes, if he had not conquered like Condé."

The respect in which Europe had till then held the
armies of Spain was now quickly transferred, as is ever
popular sentiment, to those of France. These had not for
a century gained so glorious a battle. Marignan, won by
Francis I. against the Swiss, had been as much the work of
the German mercenary bands as of the French troops.
Pavia and St. Quentin were still memories of evil omen
to Frenchmen.

Henry IV. had only won victories over his own fellow-
countrymen. Great battles, which shake dynasties, and
dwell with satisfaction for years in the memories of men,
had only hitherto in the seventeenth century been fought
and gained by Gustavus Adolphus.

The rattle of the Spanish bullets on the cuirasses of
Condé's cavalry, the fruitless discharges of the Spanish
cannon, and the loud cheers of the troopers as they
plunged sabring through the Spanish ranks that day at
Rocroi, sounded the knell of the military supremacy of
Spain, and rang in the new-born glory of France. Condé
knew not only how to conquer, but to profit by his victory.
He at once urged the government to besiege Thionville,
an important place on the Moselle which Richelieu had
long coveted, but had not as yet ventured to attempt. When
the courier who carried the news of Rocroi to the Palais
Royal returned to the camp, everything was ready for the
investment of the fortress.

Condé marched quickly through a hostile country, frus-
trated the vigilance of General Beck (August 8th, 1643), and
took Thionville. Immediately afterwards he besieged and
took Syrck, and then joined Turenne on the Upper Rhine.

Turenne, meanwhile, had pushed through the Black

Forest, and near the source of the Danube gained a success over a Bavarian detachment. For some reason which is not clear he threw a garrison into Freiburg, and retired across the Rhine. Had he remained near the town he would have prevented Mercy from investing it. So soon as Turenne was over the river, Mercy besieged Freiburg, and although Turenne advanced to relieve the place, a stupid error of some of his infantry made him fail, and Freiburg capitulated to Mercy.

When Condé met Turenne at Brisach, Freiburg had been taken, and General Mercy was entrenched under its walls with a superior army. Some counsellors recommended that he should not be attacked in front, but that a manœuvre should be made to cut off his communications. Turenne and Condé both, however, were of opinion that the intrenchments should be attacked, and thus both united in violating one of the principles of war, which rules that troops which occupy good positions in mountains, such as those of the Black Forest, should not be attacked, but outflanked, and so compelled to quit their positions. Had the French generals been content to follow this course, Mercy would have been obliged, to save his communications, gradually to retire beyond the mountains, and Freiburg would then have fallen of itself.

However, one division of Condé's army, under the command of Gramont, was hurled against the front of Mercy's entrenchments, which he had thrown up to protect his army in front of the town ; while Turenne, with the army of Weimar, made a long detour, in order to operate against the left flank of the Bavarians. The Bavarian position was strongly and gallantly held ; the action was severe. It is said that Condé threw his baton into the enemy's intrenchments, telling his troops to bring it out. Condé forced the

F

lines in front of him by dogged persistence. On the side where Turenne attacked, all night the battle raged, and in the morning he was successful, and effected his junction with Condé. But the result was inadequate to the heavy loss of men.

Both Condé and Turenne seem to have forgotten that the object of gaining a battle is not to win a few yards of ground, but to break up an enemy and force him to retreat in such disorder that his troops may be as nearly as possible annihilated in retiring. To push back an enemy in a mountain country is merely to force him from a strong position to one still stronger.

Next day, as was natural, it was found that Mercy had merely retired to a new position a little further back among the spurs of the Black Forest. The French troops were too much exhausted to attack again immediately. They had to rest all that day, and thus Mercy was allowed in quiet to entrench his new position.

On the morning after the day of repose, the two French generals reconnoitred the Bavarian lines. While they were absent on this duty, an infantry officer in Condé's army attacked without orders. The result was vexatious, for the French army was driven back with loss. Then the two generals decided to adopt the true principle of attack, and, passing to their left, turned the flank of Mercy's entrenchments, and pushed their cavalry forward to cut off his retreat into the plains beyond the mountains. The result was as might have been expected. Mercy was obliged to fall back hastily, sacrificing his cannon and baggage. He was sorely hampered and heavily punished in his retreat. Thus Condé and Turenne avenged Dutlingen. The results were not so great as they should have been, for although Mercy lost 8,000 men in his retreat, the

French had lost 9,000 in the foolhardy attack on the front of the Bavarian lines. In war every soldier lost is one cipher in the sum of the incapacity of the general.

The question now was how to take advantage of the success achieved. An ordinary or timorous captain would have adopted the obvious course of besieging Freiburg. But wider aims and broader views prevailed. Freiburg was really a place of little importance. Its garrison could easily be kept in check by the French garrison of Brisach. The army of Mercy was driven in confusion beyond the Black Forest. The French generals determined on a greater enterprise, and invested Philipsburg, which commanded a most valuable passage over the Rhine, and opened the road up the Neckar and the Tauber, which led to the rich countries and important cities that lay along the Danube, and eventually to the capital of the hereditary dominions of Austria.

During the siege Condé seized Germersheim and Spire. Turenne opened the trenches, and twelve days afterwards, on the 9th September, Philipsburg capitulated. A firm footing on the Upper Rhine was thus established. Most of the towns of the Palatinate fell immediately afterwards. Turenne took or occupied Landau, Worms, Mayence, Oppenheim, and the whole country between the Rhine and the Moselle. Condé returned to France with the army of Gramont, leaving the chief command to Turenne. His task with diminished forces was now difficult, but he carried it out ably. He had with his enfeebled army to watch over and defend a great number of places, occupied only by feeble garrisons. He had too to prepare for and resist the attacks of the Bavarians, for Mercy had reorganized his army; and when he heard of the departure of Condé, he marched on Mannheim.

Turenne succoured the towns threatened, placed a camp between Mannheim and Heidelberg, and so manœuvred that Mercy was unable to advance. The Duke of Lorraine wished to join Mercy. He passed the Moselle, and advancing to the Rhine began to besiege Baccarach. Turenne manœuvred to oppose this junction, and after some skilful marches separated the allies by occupying Kreutznach and planting his army between them. This concluded the campaign of the year. The armies retired into winter quarters. Turenne had great difficulties in feeding his men, for he had to occupy ground over which the soldiers of Lorraine—mercenary followers of a mercenary leader—had freely marched and freely plundered. As he says in his *Memoirs*, the country was so harried that it was impossible to find enough grass within twenty leagues to support a horse outside of the great towns, which were very wretched in consequence of having been the quarters of the Lorrainers. His vigilance, however, succeeded in preserving during the winter the advantages which had been gained in the campaign.

In the following year (1645) the allied Swedish and French armies continued the same faulty strategical system which had hitherto distinguished their operations against Austria. Instead of uniting in one mass, or making a concentrated attack against the capital of the hereditary dominions of the empire, they acted on separate lines disjointedly, and without affording to each other mutual support. Torstenson, who had wintered in the north of Germany at the beginning of 1645, marched into Bohemia, gained several battles, and made the Austrian ministry tremble for its capital. But his army was weakened by its own successes, and the Swedish general called from Moravia for a French advance to take the pressure of

the Imperialists off his troops. In answer to this appeal
Turenne, who had wintered in the Palatinate, passed the
Rhine at Spire by a bridge of boats, with 5,000 horsemen,
5,000 infantry, and twelve guns, and entered Wurtemburg
at the end of March. He took the field thus early because
the Bavarian army had detached about 4,000 men to reinforce the Imperial army, under Jean de Werth, who
had been defeated by Torstenson at Tabur on the 16th
March. Turenne crossed the Neckar by surprise. Mercy,
with his Bavarian force of 7,000 men, fell back. Turenne
then pushed up the Tauber, and established himself at
Marienthal, a small town on that river. The Bavarian
army appeared unable to face him. He found himself master
of all Franconia. His troops levied contributions under
the walls of Wurtzburg and Schweinfurt. Mercy had caused
the rumour to be spread that he was retiring towards the
Danube. Turenne, imposed upon by this report, and
yielding to the representations of his officers, who wished
the troops, especially the mounted corps, to be separated
for facility of subsistence, dispersed his army in cantonments around Marienthal. Mercy only waited for this.
On the second day (May 2) he rushed upon Turenne with
all his force. The French were surprised, and Turenne
himself made the serious error of fixing the point of concentration for his assembling troops in front of Marienthal
instead of in rear of the town and behind the shelter of
the Tauber. When called upon his cavalry arrived only
slowly, since, in accordance with the ignorant habits of
the time, they had seized the opportunity of a dispersion
in May to bleed their horses, and the exhausted animals
were hardly in a fit state to march. Before the army of
Turenne could be assembled the enemy was upon him, and
notwithstanding the great gallantry shown by the marshal

himself, his infantry gave way in wild confusion, and a complete rout ensued. Turenne with difficulty saved himself, and was forced to order his infantry to make their retreat as they best could to Philipsburg. Three regiments of cavalry he ordered to retire rapidly to the Main and halt on the frontiers of Hesse, a march of sixteen hours, while he himself, with two regiments of cavalry, covered the retreat, and after marching all night rejoined the main body of cavalry in Hesse.

It is a curious example of the mode in which war was conducted that the infantry, when it was broken, had no post along its line of communication where it could even rally, but had to disperse and make its flight as best it could to Philipsburg, a distance of seventy miles. In this flight of the 6,000 men of his infantry all except from 1,200 to 1,500 seem to have been lost. Notwithstanding this disaster, in which he lost all his baggage, ten guns, and 1,500 troopers, the Government did not withdraw its confidence from Turenne, although he offered to lay down his command. The Landgravine of Hesse Cassel reinforced Turenne with her own army of 6,000 men, which she put under his command, and the Swedish general Kœnigsmark, who had wintered in the bishopric of Bremen, came to his assistance with a Swedish force of 4,000 men. Turenne thus immediately after his defeat found himself at the head of an army of 14,000 soldiers, and only twelve days after his defeat at Marienthal raised the siege of Kirchheim on the frontier of Hesse, which Mercy had invested. This checked the Bavarians. They fell back, recrossed the Main, and called the Austrian corps of Gleem from Westphalia to support them.

At this time Condé was despatched by Mazarin with a little more than 7,000 men to reinforce Turenne. At the beginning of July Condé crossed the Rhine near Spire, Turenne moved into Hesse Darmstadt to meet him, and there Condé made his junction with the marshal. Condé and Turenne were thus at the head of 26,000 men, but from this soon had to be deducted 6,000 which Kœnigsmark took away from him, being unwilling to serve under Condé. Mazarin's idea was, above all things, to take some strong place in Germany, in order that the army might occupy winter quarters in that country. The French generals crossed the Neckar, took Wimpfen, near Heilbron, and thus secured a passage over the Neckar. Mercy, leaving a . strong garrison in Heilbron, retreated in all haste to Franconia. The French reached the high ground which separates the waters that flow into the Rhine from those that fall into the Danube, left Rotenbourg on the Tauber, and marched on Dinkelsbühl upon the Varnitz, which throws itself into the Danube near Donauwörth, after wandering through the plain of Nordlingen, which has often been a battle-field in European war.

Condé bore straight upon the Danube, with the desire of cutting off his opponent from the passage of that river. When he arrived near Nordlingen, he found that Mercy, by a skilful march, had almost gained Nordlingen, and was on the point of being strongly posted on the heights south of Nordlingen, which covered the road to Donauwörth. The Bavarian right occupied the hill of Weinberg. Its centre lay behind the village of Allerheim, and its left rested on a hill which rose steeply above the Eger brook. Aller heim, of which the church and cemetery were loopholed, was strongly held by infantry. Mercy's right wing consisted of Austrian cavalry, commanded by Gleem ; his left of Bavarian cavalry, commanded by Jean de Werth. Nearly

the whole of his infantry, except that which occupied the
entrenchments on the Weinberg and those on the hill near
the Eger, were posted in the village of Allerheim. So
strong was the position that Turenne was averse to the
attack, but Condé was not to be denied, and placed his
army in array. The right was under the command of
Gramont, the left under Turenne, the centre under Marsin.
At three in the afternoon (3rd August, 1645) Marsin was
ordered to advance and carry the village of Allerheim.
There a tremendous conflict arose. All Condé's infantry
was engaged without being able to force the Bavarians out
of the houses and the church, and could not be efficiently
supported by artillery fire, since in those days to move
guns was a work of great time, and artillery in position
had an enormous advantage over that which had to take
up frequently fresh ground. Condé himself rushed into
the fight, had two horses wounded and his clothes torn
into rags with bullets. Marsin was seriously wounded.
Many French officers fell. On the other side, Mercy himself was killed. The whole of the French infantry was
slain, hurt, or dispersed. The French right wing, where
Gramont commanded, was in a still worse plight. Jean
de Werth fell upon the cavalry of Gramont, although only
at a trot, as was then the pace of a charge, made the
marshal prisoner, overthrew his horsemen as well as the
reserve in rear, reached the camp and the baggage and
plundered them freely. The battle appeared to be lost,
and would certainly have been so had Werth held his
troopers in hand, and instead of allowing them to pillage,
hurled them against the flank of the still standing French
regiments, as did Cromwell his Ironsides after their victorious charge at Naseby two months previously, or Condé
at Rocroi. Condé, although wounded, hurried to Turenne,

and begged him to storm the steep slopes of Weinberg and attack Gleem, who was there intrenched. Turenne advanced under a terrible fire; Condé, with the Hessians, supported his attack; Gleem was overthrown, his guns captured, and the whole position of Weinberg carried. Turenne changed front quickly to the right, and brought his front against the right flank of the Bavarian centre, so that the Bavarian infantry in the village, finding their enemy in their rear and discouraged by the death of Mercy, were foolish enough to lay down their arms, for which Napoleon says they should have been decimated. Yet soldiers are but human beings, and cannot be expected to face certain death. They will face cheerfully desperate chances, but no sane man will face certain death. To get the best out of soldiers they must not be put into too desperate circumstances, and the general who puts his troops into such circumstances is not a strategist, but a mere gambler with the lives of men. Jean de Werth at that moment was returning from the pursuit which he had imprudently conducted too far, to a distance of four miles. Had he then moved directly to the rear of the troops of Turenne he could have reached them while still engaged in storming the Weinberg, and saved the battle. As it was, he brought back his cavalry on the direct line by which they had advanced; on regaining his former ground changed front to the left and found himself face to face with Turenne. But he was too late; order was restored in Turenne's ranks, and the battle was lost. He could do no more than retreat on Donauwörth and cross the Danube, with the loss of all his artillery.

This victory, which had a great moral effect in Germany, was dearly bought, as on the French side there fell nearly 4,000 men and many officers. The losses on the Bavarian

side were numerically about the same, but the death of
Mercy was an irreparable blow to the Bavarian cause.
Condé, to honour the memory of his adversary, whose
skill he generously appreciated, raised at Allerheim a
stone with the inscription, "*Sta, viator, heroem calcas.*"

Condé, in consequence of his victory, was able to take
Nordlingen and besiege Heilbron, but fell ill and returned
to France. Turenne remained in command of the army of
Weimar ; Gramont, who had been exchanged for Gleem,
in that of the French troops. The success at Nordlingen,
however brilliant, did not consolidate the French position
in Germany. In those days military administration was
so little understood, that when an army took the field the
duty of the Government seemed accomplished. The War
Office at home did not consider it necessary to furnish it
with reinforcements of men, money, or animals, and consequently if the front line were defeated, or even lost
heavily in a victorious battle, no resource remained but
to fall back on its base of operations. The system of
military organization by which the fighting line in front
is continually fed by reinforcements pushed up from the
rear was not thoroughly appreciated until the time of the
great Napoleon ; nor was its application thoroughly de-
velvoped until the time of Moltke. Had Napoleon, when
he advanced upon Russia, had no reserves to support his
fighting line, the disastrous retreat from Moscow to the
Vistula would have resulted in his annihilation, and he
would have found no point of security for his retreating
troops until they reached the Rhine. Had not the army
of King William, when it invaded France in 1870, received reinforcements in a continual stream from Germany,
its losses at Vionville, Gravelotte, Orleans, Le Mans, and
in front of Paris, would have prevented its carrying on

the war throughout the winter. This system of continuous reinforcement of the fighting line is one of the most important points to which the military administrator can devote his attention. Foreign countries have, in consequence of the bitter experience of late wars, laboriously turned their attention towards it, but it has not as yet received the slightest recognition from the British War Office.

For another reason, in the seventeenth century, armies, when they had been for some time in the field, were unable to continue there unless they could continually advance. The countries over which they marched were quickly devastated and exhausted. The system of supply was rude. There were no extensive trains of provision waggons to bring up food or forage from distant bases of operation, and hence we see perpetually, that although the French armies advanced into Wurtemburg and Franconia, to the banks of the Danube, and even beyond that river, they were unable to maintain themselves during the winter in the districts which they had overrun. They had to fall back to recruit and refresh themselves in Hesse Darmstadt, Hesse Cassel, on the Rhine, or in the lower Palatinate. The Swedish armies in the same way, although in the latter part of the Thirty Years' War they advanced constantly into Bohemia and Moravia, were obliged to fall back on Silesia or Bremen to subsist in winter. The Austrian and Bavarian armies had advantages over the French and Swedish, since the countries that lay along the Danube were much richer than the highlands of Wurtemburg, Franconia, or Bohemia, and they had to fall back shorter distances after each fighting season; but the principal reason why campaigns were so ineffective, why so many lives were lost and so much time exhausted fruit-

lessly, apparently, for the power engaged, and certainly
tediously for the military student, was that the system
of supply was so badly understood. It was very different
in the second half of the nineteenth century, when the
armies which besieged Paris or fought at Orleans were fed
by a magnificent supply - service along numerous roads,
and by many railways with grain that came from San
Francisco, and rice that had been exported from China.

Turenne was soon obliged to fall back on account of
want of reinforcements, want of supplies, and to be within
reach of convoys from Philipsburg. Although, when he
had received these convoys, he again advanced upon the
Upper Danube, he was again forced to retire, for the
Swedes and French, by advancing, the one through
Bohemia the other through Bavaria, gave to the Austrian Government the military advantage of interior lines.
As soon as the defeat and death of Mercy were known at
Vienna, and the Duke of Bavaria threatened to make an
independent peace with France unless he was supported,
the Archduke Leopold, relieved from the pressure of the
Swedes by their failure in the siege of Brünn and their
retreat to Silesia, was hurried up from Austria, and
marched along the southern bank of the Danube covered
by the river with 5,000 horsemen to join Jean de Werth
near Donauwörth, and oppose Turenne and Gramont.
The latter, with a reduced army and no supplies, could
do nothing but retreat. They recrossed the Neckar in
a day and a night with their whole army by swimming,
each cavalry soldier carrying an infantry man on his
saddle behind him. In those days the art of the military
engineer was so little developed that armies in the field
did not know how to form a bridge across a river, except
by means of joining together boats which could be found

in the neighbourhood. If these were absent, there was no resource for a retreating army except to swim or surrender.

Turenne retired under the ramparts of Philipsburg, hotly pursued by the Archduke, who regained Nordlingen and all the towns Turenne had conquered, and then moved into Bohemia. Turenne crossed the Rhine by a bridge of boats under cover of Philipsburg, and knowing that there were no hostile troops in Luxembourg, and that the Archduke was distant, marched suddenly upon Trèves, distant about 100 miles, dragging two guns with much difficulty over the hills of the Hundsrück for the political purpose of restoring the Elector, an ally of the French Government, who twelve years before had been driven out of his electorate.

In 1646 Turenne began his great series of strategical marches, which formed a new development in the art of war, and again introduced into military science an element which had been forgotten and eliminated since the days of the ancients. He advanced from the Moselle, where his army had lain in winter quarters round Trèves, early in May, and threw a bridge of boats over the Rhine at Baccarach. The error by which the Swedes operated on one line against the Austrians and Bavarians, and the French on another, had now become apparent, and it was resolved that the Swedes should unite with the army of Turenne, and that these both together should push forward towards the Danube. To effect their junction, the Swedish army under Wrangel, who had replaced Torstenson, as the latter had been forced to return to Sweden on account of a bad gout, drew down to the frontiers of Hesse Darmstadt. Turenne purposed to cross the Rhine at Baccarach and join them in Hesse. When he was ready to advance he suddenly received orders from Mazarin to stand fast, since

the Duke of Bavaria had promised that he would not join
the army of the Austrians, but would remain neutral provided that the French did not cross the Rhine. Notwithstanding this assurance the Bavarians joined the Austrians,
and with them pushed forward so as to prevent Turenne
effecting his junction with the Swedes by his bridge at
Baccarach. When the infidelity of the Bavarians became
apparent, it was too late to join the Swedes directly, and
the bridge of boats had been destroyed by a sudden flood.
There was no other passage across the Rhine higher up
than Wesel, which lay 160 miles down the stream.
Turenne, however, quickly took his resolve. Two days
after he knew of the march of the enemy, he broke up
from Baccarach, marched down the Rhine to Wesel,
obtained permission from the Dutch Government to cross
there, and then marched up the Rhine again on the right
bank to Friedberg in Hesse, where he joined the Swedes.
This was a march of 320 miles, which was accomplished in
a little more than a month. On the 10th of August
Turenne met Wrangel, whom the Imperialists had not
meanwhile ventured to attack, on account of his strong
positions which he had taken up near Friedberg. Their
united force mustered 10,000 horsemen, 6,000 foot, and
60 guns. The day after joining the Swedes the French
army took up the duties of advanced guard. Such a march
has seldom been equalled except by Crawford's light
division, when it hurried up to Talavera. Turenne and
Wrangel had no jealousy, no differences. They worked
well together. The enemy lay in front of them with
14,000 horsemen, 10,000 foot, and 50 guns. Turenne
informed the Duke of Bavaria that in consequence of
having violated his engagement with France, he intended
to meet him as an enemy.

The question now arose as to the line on which it might be most advantageous to carry on the war. It was at first suggested that it might be well to move leaving Frankfurt on the left along the Upper Rhine into Baden, but the result of this movement would only have been to drive the enemy back upon the rich countries of Suabia and Franconia, where they would have better quarters in the following winter than those which the French and Swedes would enjoy. In those days good winter quarters were of great importance, as not only must an army which could not find supplies in the country that it had occupied fall back on richer lands in rear, but the mercenary levies that were disbanded in the autumn always joined the army which was in the best winter quarters.

A brilliant movement was determined upon. The Swedes and French moved towards Frankfurt, seized the passages of the small streams north of the Main, pushed up the Main itself, and drove the Imperialists away from that river. Thus the French gained the direct road up the Tauber to the Danube, while the Imperialists were pushed back to the distant and circuitous route by way of Nuremberg and Bamberg; Aschaffenberg was quickly taken; Schorndorf, an important fortress, fell in three days. The Swedes, marching on the left, took Nordlingen, and quickly reached Donauwörth, where they crossed the Danube, while at the same time Turenne seized Lauingen on the same river. The Swedes pushed forward (22nd September), crossed the Lech at Rain where it falls into the Danube, and invested the place. Turenne advanced, besieged Augsburg, and sent his couriers to levy contributions at the very gates of Munich.

The Swedes had, on the line of communications, garrisoned Nordlingen and Donauwörth, and the French

Lauingen, so that these lines were tolerably secure. Turenne was persuaded by Wrangel to give up the siege of Augsburg, and to join in pushing that of Rain, which was only held by raw levies. He heard, during his absence, that a strong garrison was thrown into Augsburg which showed the error of making the siege of Rain instead of Augsburg, the main and most important object. Rain was soon delivered up by its garrison, who had fired a great deal but defended themselves very badly. Augsburg was then besieged.

In the meantime the Archduke, having fallen back by way of Bamberg and Nuremberg, crossed the Danube, and raised the siege of Augsburg, The French and Swedes fell back on Lauingen which they fortified. The Archduke crossed the Lech at Landsberg, above Augsburg, and began to move by way of Meiningen towards Ulm in the hopes of forcing the allies, through want of supplies, to retire, so that in the winter he could regain Nordlingen, Donauwörth, and the other fortresses which they had taken and garrisoned. Turenne now made some brilliant movements. He made a feint as of marching towards Ulm. Then suddenly turned, moved direct on Landsberg, seized the Archduke's bridge over the Lech and his magazines, and cut off the Imperialists' communication with Munich, which was at once menaced by the French cavalry, and with the hereditary dominions. The Archduke was thus forced to fall back into Upper Bavaria, while Turenne seized at the same time all the supplies and provisions which the Austrian commissaries had collected at Augsburg. The Duke of Bavaria, separated from his army, was forced by this campaign to make proposals of peace. The Archduke marched by a circuitous route towards Regensburg, in order not so much to secure winter

quarters as to get beyond striking distance of the allies.
A great opportunity was now available to Turenne to
carry the war into the heart of the hereditary dominions,
but a strong party at the French court objected to pushing
hostilities to an extremity, since they were afraid that
the fall of Austria would mean the fall of the Catholic
party in Germany, and that the Swedes would impose
upon the Catholics such conditions as they chose. This
was indeed an error, for France would have been as
powerful to defend the Catholic cause in Germany as she
was to invade the hereditary dominions of the emperor.
Bavaria quickly made peace, and promised the passage of
troops and provisions through her territory if the French
wished to invade Austria. The emperor, after having
separated from the Bavarian army, had a force of only
5,000 foot and 6,000 horse at his disposal, while the French
and Swedes had 14,000 foot and 20,000 cavalry. Turenne
was prepared to invade Austria, but the snow and frost
of a severe winter compelled him to go into winter
quarters, and prevented him from taking advantage of his
opportunity before the close of 1646. Peace was concluded between France and Bavaria 14th March, 1647.
The Austrian army retired from the Bavarian territory
into Austria. The court of France, unwilling to make the
Swedes too powerful, or to carry out the total subjugation
of Austria, withdrew the French troops from the valley of
the Danube. These were required too in Flanders. Condé,
who had taken Dunkirk in 1646, and first given it to
France, had caused some jealousy to the court by his
brilliant successes. He had been sent to Catalonia with
a considerable part of his army, and was now engaged
on the fruitless siege of Lerida. Against the order to
move to Flanders and to sacrifice the great opportunity of

G

striking a deadly blow against the house of Austria,
Turenne remonstrated in vain.   He was peremptorily
ordered to march, although he pointed out that probably
his German cavalry, to whom five months' pay was due,
might make some difficulty about moving into Flanders.
He marched his army to Philipsburg, there crossed the
Rhine, and advanced to Saverne, which was then regarded
as the frontier town between France and Germany.
Further, the German cavalry, who declared that they were
only engaged to fight in Germany, would not move.   A
mutiny ensued, which Turenne suppressed with great
coolness, vigour, and determination, but not without
having to pursue the retreating cavalry as far as Konig-
shofen, on the Tauber, where he had to charge them and
break them up.   Some returned to their duty, others
joined the Swedes.   With the troops he could collect
Turenne marched into Luxembourg, where he made demon-
strations which caused the Imperialists to send a detachment of about 5,000 men to watch him.   In the meantime
the Bavarians broke their treaty with France and entered
into active alliance with Austria.   The Archduke advanced,
taking advantage of Turenne being unable to oppose him,
and laid siege to Worms, driving back the Swedes into
Brunswick.   Turenne was accordingly ordered to return
to Germany.   He raised the siege of Worms, and was
ready to join with the Swedes and push forward again
against the Imperialists, but the Swedes had been so mal-
treated that they needed time to restore their cavalry, and
were unable to resume the field that winter.   Turenne was
obliged to retire to Strasbourg, without striking any
blow.   There he refitted his army.

He obtained horses from Switzerland to recruit his
cavalry, and on the 11th February, 1648, crossed the

Rhine at Mayence, and marched to join the Swedes in Franconia, although through a devastated country where he could not even obtain hay to feed his horses. With care for the comfort of his infantry, who had hitherto been much neglected in war, he had cloaks made for them to protect them from the wintry weather. His force was 4,000 foot, 4,000 horse, and 20 guns. Turenne marched up the Main, joined the Swedes in Franconia on the 23rd March, and the united armies crossed to the southern bank of the Main. The Bavarians and Imperialists were at Ingoldstadt, the French and Swedes at Rothenburg on the Tauber, when operations began. The Austrians marched upon Ulm with the intention of moving towards the Rhine. Turenne and the Swedes quickly marched against them, reached Lauingen, where there was a French garrison, and there came in contact with the head of the Imperial columns (17th May). These retreated, and in covering their retreat General Melander, who commanded the rear guard of Piccolomini, was killed, and his troops driven off, although only after a gallant resistance which saved the Imperial army from destruction, and allowed it to retire across the Lech at Augsburg. Turenne pushed on upon Rain (19th May), where he forced the passage of the Lech in exactly the same place as Gustavus had forced it in 1632, when opposed by Tilly. The enemy retreated, and crossed the Isar at Freising. Turenne occupied Freising. The Imperialists retired to the Inn, throwing garrisons into Munich, Wasserburg, and Ingoldstadt. The Duke of Bavaria fled from Munich to Salsburg. Turenne advanced to the Isar and then to the Inn. There were no boats, and although the French tried to cross at Wessembourg, Mühldorf, and other points, they were unable to do so. Thus, Turenne was the first of French generals who planted

the colours of France upon the Inn. Here he stayed
fifteen days, and harried Upper Bavaria in a manner
which has been regarded as a reproach to his memory.
The Imperialists, who had been meanwhile reinforced by
large levies, restored their armies at Passau, and crossed
to the northern bank of the Danube at that place under
Piccolomini, threatening to cut the French communications
with the Rhine. Turenne and the Swedes fell back from
the Inn to the Isar at Dingolfing. Here they were stayed,
as they could not pass the river, but the Swedes made a
bridge of piles, and the French officers for the first time
then learnt from the Swedes how to make a field bridge
without boats. For four weeks the opponent armies
manœuvred on the Isar. In the meantime a detachment
of the Swedish army, which after the death of Melander
had been sent against Prague, had taken that place, and
was pushing forwards towards Vienna.

Affairs had not during the year stood still in Flanders.
Condé had been called back to that theatre of war on
account of the progress made by the Imperialists. The
Archduke Leopold, brother of Ferdinand III., had besieged Lens in Artois. Condé gained a brilliant victory
and raised the siege on the 20th August. This catastrophe,
and Turenne's raid to the Inn, urged Austria to seek for
the peace which was absolutely necessary for her. Negotiations were more promptly pushed forward at Munster.
Turenne retired with his army to Swabia and the Swedes
to Nuremberg.

Since Turenne had been made a Marshal of France the
course of war had consistently gone against Spain and the
empire in all quarters. In 1644 the Duke of Orleans, a
worthy son of Henry IV., had taken Gravelines, Courtrai,
Mardyck. In 1645 Albuquerque, with his Portuguese, had

won a great victory over the Spaniards at Badajoz. The victories of Turenne and Condé we have already followed. Austria was everywhere worsted, and accordingly the peace of Westphalia was signed at Munster on the 24th October, which for more than a century established the national law of Europe.

The Spaniards did not enter into this peace with France, for they trusted to other circumstances to allow them to inflict a heavy blow upon the kingdom, and Spanish policy was partly right, for although the armies of France had gained many victories, internal discord was at work within the country itself, and few of the advantages which ought to have been reaped from the successful campaigns of Turenne and Condé really accrued to their country.

By the peace of Westphalia France gained on the left bank of the Rhine, Metz, Toul, Verdun, the whole of Alsace, and the Sundgau, or country south of Mulhausen ; on the right bank, Brisach and the protectorates of Philipsburg, with the right there of garrison and passage. The sovereignty of the place remained with the Elector of Trèves in his capacity as Bishop of Spire. No fort was to be erected on the right bank of the Rhine between Bale and Philipsburg by either party, nor was the course of the river to be changed. France paid Austria 3,000,000 livres, and undertook the charge of two-thirds of the debt of Alsace. The emperor surrendered Montferrat, and renounced his rights over Pinerolo, which the Duke of Savoy had ceded to Lewis XIII. by the treaty of St. Germain in 1632. Sweden became the most important power in the north, and formed a portion of the Germanic body. She obtained the town of Wismar, the island of Rugen, Pomerania, and the bishoprics of Bremen and Verden, which had been secularised, with three votes in the Diet.

The Elector Palatine recovered the Lower Palatinate, and an eighth electorate was created in his favour. The other allies of France, the Elector of Saxony, the Duke of Mecklenburgh, the Landgraf of Hesse-Cassel, and the Duke of Brunswick, received territorial indemnities taken from Catholic domains. The Dukes of Savoy, of Mantua, and Modena, recovered all such portions of their states as had been taken from them by Spain. France recognised the independence of Holland and Switzerland. The religious liberty established by the peace of Augsburg was maintained, and the Calvinists were admitted to equal rights with the Lutherans. The federal constitution of Germany was confirmed, extended, and placed under the guarantee of France and Sweden. The emperor was subordinated to the Diet, and a voice given to the princes and the states of Germany in all the affairs of the empire, such as alliances, treaties, and wars. The emperor retained only an executive power. France now had not only gained a frontier on the Upper Rhine and a natural defence against Germany, but French preponderance was established in the empire and in Europe. This peace and its conditions which were so favourable to France were due to Mazarin, Condé, and Turenne.

CHAPTER VI.

THE FRONDE.

SPAIN did not enter into the peace of Westphalia. The ministry of Madrid had, at the beginning of the negotiations, concluded a separate peace with Holland. Civil discord had begun in France. The Spanish government hoped to profit from the internal divisions of the kingdom. Mercenaries disbanded in Germany flocked to the Spanish standards; and the emperor, notwithstanding the peace, allowed troops who owed allegiance to the house of Austria to take service in Flanders.

Anne of Austria, absolute regent, made Mazarin master of France. He held over her the command which an able man acquires over a woman sufficiently weak to be ruled and sufficiently firm to persist in her choice. At first the cardinal used his power with a moderation, and with a simplicity as marked as Richelieu had shown pride. The queen wished to make her regency respected. Gaston, Duke of Orleans, brother of Lewis XIII., and the Prince of Condé, supported her power, and it appeared that the nobility now had no desire except to serve the state.

Taxes had been necessary, however, to support the war against Spain and against the empire. The finances of

France since the death of Henry IV. had been as badly
managed as those of England, of Spain, or of Germany.
Peculation was rampant, but the revenue in the first years
of the regency amounted to 75,000,000*l.* It was enough
had economy been observed in the administration, but this
was not so, and in 1746-47 there was need of further supplies. We have already seen how the troops of Weimar
were kept five months in arrear of their pay, and how this
want of pay led to their mutiny when ordered to Flanders.
The other troops of the army were equally in arrear.
Mazarin's superintendent of finance was also an Italian
named Emeri, whose prodigality and debauchery were the
scorn of Paris. To raise supplies this fellow created ridicu-
lous and burdensome imposts. He sold letters of nobility.
He created offices of comptrollers of firewood and sworn
sellers of hay.

The *octroi* duties of Paris were raised, and the salaries
of the magistracy were reduced. It is easy to imagine how
the French were irritated against two Italians who had
both come to France without means, and had become rich
at the cost of the nation, when these established taxes
which cost them both expense and inconvenience. The
parliament of Paris and the other courts and the burghers
of the capital loudly murmured. It was in vain that
Mazarin removed Emeri from his charge, and ordered him to
retire to one of his estates. Men were angered that such
a man still had estates in France, and Cardinal Mazarin
became odious and unpopular, although at this very time
he was carrying out the great work of the peace of
Westphalia.

Voltaire scornfully remarks that the civil wars began at
Paris as those which had just finished in England began,
for the sake of a little money ; but under this question of a

little money there lay great constitutional principles. Had there been in England, as there was now in France, an exclusive and haughty nobility, the younger sons of which never descended into the middle classes, and which was never recruited from the middle classes, either by marriage or promotion ; had there been such a nobility, which never became connected with the men of arts, arms, or letters ; had there existed in England—as there existed in France and in Spain—a separate noble caste, which has been the curse of all countries, and the ruin of most, the parliament of Westminster might have gradually fallen as feebly under the domination of the house of Stuart as that of Paris—which was at this time more bold, more respected, and more formidable than that of Charles I.—fell under the house of Bourbon ; but fortunately the Wars of the Roses and the prowess of English archers had almost exterminated in England the great feudal houses. Fortunately the Commons of England had the will to demand their rights and the power to maintain them in face of both coronet and crown. The middle classes, both in boroughs and counties, free from the dead weight of an idle aristocracy, had been raised to a power in the state. The armies of the new model, which served under Cromwell and Fairfax, were recruited from yeomen and freeholders, and were formed of well-paid and well-to-do men, with property and interest in the country. They were as different from the sweepings of the feudal estates, which were carelessly ordered into the field by Bouillon, and slavishly followed Beaufort, as are the corporals of our regiments of Lifeguards or the Volunteers of the Inns of Court from the roughs of Ratcliff Highway.

The parliament of Paris at first opposed the edicts of Mazarin, and gained the confidence of the people. Neither in France nor in England did the disputes between the crown and the power of the purse lead at once to armed revolt. A mob may rush to arms or raise barricades in a moment of excitement, but men accustomed to consider and decide weighty matters of state, act with more caution, and endeavour to observe propriety even at the most exciting moments.

By remitting taxes to the members of the parliament itself, Mazarin hoped to overcome opposition, but the parliament was too wise to prefer its own interest to that of the people at large. It demanded that the superintendents of taxes, who had been established under Lewis XIII., should be abolished, and desired that according to the ancient laws no citizen should be thrown into prison unless his natural judges should be made acquainted with the fact within twenty-four hours. Here was a French Habeas Corpus Act, but how differently was it observed in France to England, as *lettres de cachet* and the Bastile abundantly witnessed.

These disputes were at their height when Condé won his great victory at Lens (20th August, 1648). The king, who was a boy of ten years old, on hearing of the battle, remarked, "The parliament will be terribly vexed." At that time the court regarded the parliament of Paris only as an assemblage of rebels, and by talking of them in this strain made their rebellion more imminent. Notwithstanding the example of a neighbouring country, the queen and the cardinal resolved to seize three of the most disobedient members, and to terrify the people by causing them to be arrested in the fulness of day, while at Notre Dame a *Te Deum* was being chanted for the victory of Lens, and at the very moment when the porters were bringing into the church seventy-three standards taken from the enemy.

This caused the shock that shook the kingdom to its foundation. Two of the members escaped, one was arrested and carried away towards Sedan. The seizure of Broussil, far from intimidating the people, irritated and roused them. Shops were shut, chains of iron were stretched across the principal streets, barricades were erected, and 400,000 voices shouted for the freedom and liberty of Broussil.

The queen ordered 2,000 men of the troops which were billeted some miles from Paris up to the capital, to support the household brigade. But a new figure appeared upon the scene. Paul de Gondi, Coadjutor of Paris, famous afterwards under the name of Cardinal de Retz, placed himself at the head of the revolution. The chancellor, attacked by the people, was with difficulty conveyed by two companies of musqueteers and a squad of gendarmes to the Palais Royal. More and more barricades were erected and were pushed to within 100 paces of the Palais Royal itself. The soldiers, after losing a few men under the fire of the populace, fell back and looked on quietly at the proceedings. The parliament went in procession to the queen through the barricades, which were levelled before them, and demanded its imprisoned member. The queen was obliged to yield, and thus invited fresh outrages.

Anne of Austria could not appear in public without being insulted. The people called her Dame Anne, and if any other title were added it was one of opprobrium. She was accused of sacrificing the state to her friendship for Mazarin ; and when she went abroad, over the heads of her guards and through the intervals in their files, she heard on every side songs, witticisms, and coarse buffoonery, which cast rude reproach upon her character and threw doubts on her virtue. Worn out by annoyances she fled

from Paris with her children, her minister, the Duke of
Orleans, brother of Lewis XIII., and the great Condé
himself, and settled, a refugee, at Saint Germain, where
nearly the whole of the court had to sleep upon straw.
She was forced to pawn the crown jewels to get money
(6th January, 1649). The king wanted the most necessary articles; his pages were sent away, as they could not
be fed. The aunt of Lewis XIV., daughter of Henry,
wife of the King of England, a refugee at Paris, was there
reduced to the direst poverty, and her daughter, afterwards
married to the brother of Lewis XIV., had to remain in
bed because she had no fuel with which to warm herself.
Without, the people of Paris were angered and furious,
paying no attention to the afflictions of so many royal per-
sonages. The Queen Regent of France and the Queen of
England are two memorable examples of the reverses
which may fall upon crowned heads.

Anne of Austria, with tears in her eyes, urged Condé
to act as protector of the kingdom. The hero of Rocroi,
Freibourg, Lens, and Nordlingen, was flattered with the
honour of defending a court, although he considered it un·
grateful, against the rebellion, which also invoked his aid.
The parliament and its party, which was known as La
Fronde, had the great Condé to resist, but it did not fear
the contest.

We have seen before that at the time of the conspiracy of
Cinq Mars and the treaty with Spain, the Duke of Bouillon
had been arrested, and Sedan had been taken from him.
We know, too, that this conspiracy had been formed by
the duke and the queen against their common enemy,
Richelieu; that Bouillon had generously offered Sedan as
an asylum for the queen from Richelieu and the king, and
had sworn to die in defending her. He had been ruined

for her. At the beginning of the new reign he naturally expected recompense for his services in the shape of the restoration of his patrimony, and failed to perceive that the sentiments of Anne when regent should be different from those when she had been the victim of Richelieu. On the other hand, Anne herself, on assuming the reins of power, knew better than any one that Sedan was a place of the utmost importance; that for twenty years it had been the centre of all the plots formed against the royal authority; that in case of need it might become, as in former times, a place for the concentration of foreign troops intended to invade France. Thus Sedan could not be restored to the family of Auvergne without compromising the safety of the state; but it could have been kept, and honourably kept, if the ejected family had been at once compensated fairly for the loss of its property. Mazarin was too subtle, and Anne too careless, to deal promptly and liberally with the duke. Although since 1643 he had been promised compensation for the place, in 1649 nothing had been settled.

When the Fronde broke out, the Prince of Conti, brother of Condé, the Duke of Longueville, the Duke of Beaufort, and the Duke of Bouillon adopted the party of the coadjutor and the parliament. Generals were chosen for an army with which to resist the court. Although taxes levied by Mazarin had been resisted, taxes were freely paid to raise troops—12,000 men were raised; Condé had 8,000 soldiers. These he threw around Paris, and invested 100,000 burgesses, and threatened to starve the town. The citizens, adorned with feathers and ribbons, made sorties occasionally, but their manœuvres were the subject of scorn by the soldiers. They fled when they met 200 men of the regular troops, and when they returned always worsted, they were received in the streets with hooting and shouts of laughter.

Public-houses were the tents where councils were held, in the midst of jokes, songs, and the most dissolute gaiety. The coadjutor-archbishop of Paris took his seat in parliament with a poignard in his pocket, and when its hilt was seen the whole house shouted, " There is the breviary of our archbishop." A messenger from the court arrived at the gate of St. Antoine with proposals of accommodation. The parliament would not receive him, but it admitted an envoy of the Archduke Leopold who was carrying on war against France.

As Voltaire says, the tone of the civil discords which afflicted England at the same time mark well the difference between the national characters. The English had thown into their civil war a balanced fury and a mournful determination. Scaffolds were erected for the conquered. The king taken prisoner was brought before a court of justice, questioned on the abuses which he had allowed to be done in his name, condemned to lose his head, and executed in the face of the people. The French on the other hand threw themselves into their civil strife with caprice, laughter, dissolution, and debauchery. Women were the leaders of factions—love made and broke cabals. The Duchess of Longueville urged Turenne, only a short time back appointed Marshal of France, to encourage his army to revolt, which he was commanding for his king. Nothing can justify Turenne's action in this matter. Had he laid down his command and taken the side of his brother on account of his family grievance, the feudal spirit which in those days held affection for family higher than affection for country, might have excused him; but while in the service of a sovereign and intrusted with the command

of an army, to endeavour to lead his troops over to the
enemy can be regarded as nothing short of the work of a
traitor. He himself pleads as his apology that Condé was
starving the population of Paris by the investment, but
we can hardly accept as an excuse that his feelings were
so harrowed by the hunger of the citizens that he would
betray the trust confided in him, when we consider the
manner in which under his command Bavaria and the
Palatinate were treated during some of his campaigns.
Neither can it be an excuse for him when it was alleged
that Mazarin had sent to Italy for his own private investment the money which should have paid his troops for
the five months due to them. Had he suspected such procedure the duty of Turenne was to lay the matter before
the court. As it was he sacrificed his honour, and allowed
his fair fame to be tarnished for the sake of a worthless
woman who secretly jeered at his passion, and cared
nothing for his heart, but merely for his sword for her own
worldly advantage. ' As it was he endeavoured to persuade
his army to declare for the parliament, and purposed
taking it into Champagne, and marching for the relief of
the capital ; but the treachery of the marshal was no
match for the subtlety of the cardinal. Before Turenne
issued his declaration to his troops the colonels of his
regiment had already been tampered with. The cardinal's
emissaries had promised them pensions, and distributed
800,000*l.* among the officers and soldiers. This was a
decisive argument for mercenaries, who taught Turenne
by forsaking him that mercenary services can only be
commanded by money. D'Erlach had also stood firm.
The regiments of Turenne, six German regiments, called
by d'Erlach, marched one night to join him at Brisach.
Three regiments of infantry threw themselves under the

guns of Philipsburg. Only a small force was left to
Turenne, who, finding the blow he intended hopeless, sent
the troops still with him to join d'Erlach at Brisach, and
retired himself with fifteen or twenty of his friends to
Heilbron, thence to Holland, where he awaited the termination of the civil war. The news of the abandonment
of Turenne was received with despair at Paris, with wild
joy at St. Germain. His banishment, however, was not
long.

The leaders of the parliament became aware that the
princes of the Fronde were trying to obtain foreign
assistance to overturn the monarchy ; that their generals
were negotiating a treaty with Spain. They felt that
order, peace, and the independence of parliament, which
would in this case become dependent upon the nobility, was
in danger. They took the patriotic resolution quickly to
act of their own accord. A conference had been opened
between the parliament and the court. Peace was concluded at Reuil, which, notwithstanding the remonstrances
of Conti, Bouillon, and the other nobles of the Fronde, was
accepted by the whole parliament. Peace was proclaimed
in Paris to the discontent of the populace. The leaders
of the parliament, disgusted with the conduct of the
nobles, made no stipulation in this treaty on their behalf,
except an annuity and some vain promises for which no
guarantees were given.

Turenne, on the conclusion of the treaty of Reuil,
embarked in Zeeland, landed at Dieppe, and posted to
Paris. There he found the nobles naturally discontented,
the Prince of Conti irritated because he had not received
honours proportionate to his services, and had been refused
the command of the army in Flanders. The court was
occupied with the campaign, which led to nothing worthy

of note but the raising of the siege of Cambrai. Condé, who did not this year command in Flanders, but instead made a journey into Burgundy on his return to Paris, took the lead in ridiculing Mazarin, insulting the government, and braving the queen. He joined with his brother Conti and the Duke of Longueville, and became the head of the party which was known as *" Les petits maîtres " ;* they wished to be masters of the state. This name is still current in the French language as a memorial of the troubles of the Fronde, and is now applied to the rich and ignorant youth who flaunt the boulevards of Paris and encircle the stage doors of its theatres.

The nobles, while loudly asserting public right, sought each to establish his own fortune on public ruin. Gaston was jealous of the glory of Condé and of his successes. Mazarin again succeeded by a doubtful wile. He obtained the signature of Condé to the seizure of certain conspirators who were alleged to have plotted Condé's assassination, and under the authority of this warrant, Condé, his brother Conti, and his brother-in-law Longueville, were arrested (18th January, 1650), because Mazarin feared them, and lodged prisoners in Vincennes; and so doubtful is popular feeling, that the same people of Paris who had shouted for joy over Rocroi and Lens, fired salvoes in delight when the defender and hero of France was conducted to his dungeon.

But this seizure, which was intended to stamp out revolt, raised revolution. The mother of Condé presented a petition to parliament, his wife fled to Bordeaux, aided by the Duke of Rochefoucauld, raised this town, and sought assistance from Spain. A design was quickly made to deliver the princes, but one of those intrusted with the plan confessed to a priest, who carried the

H

information to the coadjutor, who had now joined the Court and was the enemy of Condé. Turenne, who on his return to France had become closely intimate with Condé, and who was still so beloved by his soldiers that they had refused to obey d'Erlach, and requested he should be again placed at their head, was also intended to be seized by the cardinal. He succeeded in escaping, however; and while his brother took refuge in Turenne, where he became one of the leaders of the civil war, Turenne himself fled to Stenay on the Meuse, which he held for Condé, where he was joined by Madame de Longueville, and where he took measures to force the court to relasee the prince.

Condé's cause, abandoned by the people and parliament, was warmly espoused by the nobility. The first act of the drama of civil commotion had passed. The struggle was no longer between the parliament and the court for the rights of the people, but a struggle between the nobility and the prime minister for place and power. The period of the young Fronde began a period in which woman played the greater part. The two princesses of Condé showed themselves as skilful and enterprising on the one side as Madame de Chevreuse, the adviser of Anne of Austria, on the other. The princesses went to the castle of Montrond, then to the castle of Turenne, rousing the people, receiving hospitality, and urging the release of their kinsmen. The Duchess of Longueville was a heroine of romantic enterprise, which might lead her to be classed as an adventuress. After having endeavoured in vain to raise Normandy, she reached Holland by sea on board of an English vessel, and thence flew to Stenay, where Turenne had been waiting her for a month—if one may believe the memoirs of the time—with an impatience which

cannot be entirely attributed solely to his interest in
politics. Turenne at Stenay styled himself lieutenant-
general for the delivery of the princes. He worked to
collect troops, communicated with all the governors of the
provinces whom he judged discontented with the court,
sent messengers to the camps where the troops were
billeted who had served under him in Germany, and three
regiments from Lorraine joined him at Stenay; but Mazarin
by force of money and energy was able to hold the greater
part of the troops on the side of the court. Turenne was
then forced to seek for aid elsewhere. He turned to Spain,
and after several conferences with a Spanish envoy at
Montmedy a treaty was concluded (20th April, 1650)
between the court of Spain on the one side, and Turenne
and Madame de Longueville on the other. The latter engaged not to lay down arms until Condé was released from
prison, and until a just and reasonable peace should be
afforded to Spain; 5,000 Spaniards were placed under the
order of the marshal, and Spain also undertook to furnish
garrisons for fortresses on the frontier that might be taken.
In consequence of this treaty war was prepared for. Turenne
doubtless in this case also committed a crime in leaguing
himself with the enemies of his country, and in agreeing
to place in their hands its frontier fortresses and the gates
of its capital. The skill of Mazarin never shone so brightly
as in the steps he took to overcome the difficulties which
now rose around him. He laboured to pacify the kingdom
after having pacified Paris. He quickly journeyed through
the provinces which were most uneasy, such as Normandy,
Burgundy, and Guyenne, everywhere getting the better of
the rebels either by skilful negotiation or by force of
arms. The whole of the year 1650 he devoted to this
work. At the same time he watched Turenne and his

allies in the north, and with movements of troops succeeded
in holding them in check.

After the treaty with Spain the Spaniards wished to
pour into Picardy, while the marshal with his troops was
to occupy Champagne and hold in check the forces which
France might detach to check the Spanish invasion. These
covered in their advance by Turenne might have had no
anxiety in their conquests, and in a short time would have
gained the fruit of the alliance, but Turenne was honest
even in his infidelity. He would not cause the ruin of his
country, and perceiving the object of the Spaniards was to
conquer the French territory more than to free Condé,
opposed it firmly. He invariably asserted that the aim of
the alliance was to obtain the liberty of the princes and
lead to a general peace, and to this end alone his efforts
must be directed; that it was necessary to march to the
gates of Vincennes, and to do so all the forces available
must be united.

The archduke and the marshal assumed the offensive
in July, attacked La Capelle, besieged Guise, whence they
were forced to retire through famine, took La Capelle,
and marched on Vervins. Turenne then took Château
Porcien and Rethel, where he left a garrison under Delli-
ponti. He then wished to march on Paris. Hocquincort,
who endeavoured to bar his way, was defeated at Fisnes
and pursued to the gates of Soissons, and the main part
of the king's army was shut up in Rheims. Wild confusion burst forth at Paris, but the blow that was intended
was defeated, for the princes were suddenly removed from
Vincennes to Havre.

So soon as Turenne saw his hope of freeing them dis-
appointed he retired from the neighbourhood of Paris and
rejoined the archduke. The allies then invested Mouzon

on the Meuse, about five miles from Stenay, to assure a
good passage of that river and obtain wider winter quarters
in this direction. During the siege Turenne commanded
the covering army between the Meuse and the Aisne.

Mouzon fell early in November. A portion of the
allied army took up its winter quarters in Flanders, while
Turenne remained on the Meuse with 8,000 men and six
guns.

While these events passed in the north Mazarin nego-
tiated with the people of Bordeaux and granted them a
full amnesty on the condition that the king and his troops
should enter the town. The Princess of Condé, the Dukes
of Bouillon and Rochefoucauld, with other partisans, were
allowed to retire to their properties. The conditions of
the arrangement were light, but money was much wanting
to the government. The coadjutor was also again restless
and was stirring up the Duke of Orleans to seize the
direction of affairs. Since Guyenne was pacified Mazarin
made his arrangements to establish order in Provence and
Catalonia, brought the court to Fontainebleau, where he
prepared for a campaign against Turenne and the
Spaniards.

At Rheims in December he was active in the concentration of troops and the collection of munitions, and on the 9th
of that month, Marshal Plessis, moving by way of Verdun
by his orders, suddenly besieged Rethel, where Turenne had
left a garrison of 1,800 men. Under the eyes of Mazarin
the siege works were pushed with such vigour that the
town capitulated before the middle of the month, although
the governor had been informed that Turenne was coming
to relieve him. Turenne did indeed, after four days' march,
arrive in front of Rethel, a few hours only after the capitulation. Learning by the reports of the prisoners whom

he took from the hostile cavalry that he was too late, and
not wishing with an army fatigued and inferior in number
to attack a victorious force, he retreated. Plessis pursued,
and Turenne made the great error of halting to deliver
battle when no object could be gained by it, since Rethel
had already fallen. The force under Plessis was double
that which he commanded. To cover a large front he
'formed no reserve, and although he did all that personal
gallantry could to save the battle, the Spaniards surrounded
on all sides were almost cut to pieces, and Turenne himself,
with his horse shot in five places, had the greatest difficulty
in escaping. His own regiment, which had refused quarter,
had all its officers and soldiers either killed or captured.

Affairs were now desperate for the viscount. He retired to Bar-le-Duc, then to Montmedy, where he rallied
the remains of his army, and after a certain time returned
to Stenay and rejoined Madame de Longueville.

Mazarin took every advantage of his victory, regained
the fortresses which had been taken, and thus freed
Champagne from the enemy. At the same time Normandy,
Burgundy, and Guyenne were reduced to obedience.

The princes and nobles had now no strongholds except
Stenay and Montrond. The cardinal's prospects were
brilliant. He could legitimately hope for the conclusion
of a final and glorious peace with Spain as well as the
establishment of order in the interior of the country.

But at this moment he suddenly found himself face to
face with great embarrassment. Gondi, who had not obtained his cardinal's hat, renewed his intrigues with Anne
of Gonzaga, who, as famous for her beauty and gallantry
of her youth as renowned for her wit and charm of con-
versation, wished to bestow on Condé something besides a
platonic devotion. She conceived the idea of uniting the

parliament and the partisans of the princes in a great league against Mazarin. She took the coadjutor into her confidence, and at the moment when the cardinal was dreaming of forming in France a great monarchical and national party for the establishment of order, they arranged an agreement (4th February, 1641) between the parliament and the Fronde.

The agreement was signed in the house of the princess palatine. Parliament voted that the queen should be requested as soon as possible to grant freedom to the princes and to banish Mazarin, to whom were imputed all the calamities of the kingdom. The citizens of Paris, by the orders of the Duke of Orleans, took arms, seized the gates of the town, and Mazarin, fearful of becoming a victim to popular vengeance, fled from Paris in the night. He retired to Havre, where he released the princes, but naturally met with the disdain from them which he might have expected. He then retired to Sedan, thence to Liege, and finally to Cologne.

While Mazarin, a proscribed fugitive, hurried over the frontier, Condé re-entered Paris amidst the acclamations of the same people who had so much applauded his imprisonment a year before. He appeared in parliament to thank that body for what it had done, and some days afterwards parliament passed acts which annulled all the declarations of treason and forfeiture which had previously been passed against the Duchess of Longueville, Turenne, the Duke of Bouillon, Rochefoucauld, and all those who had supported the cause of the princes. The queen was forced to accept at the same time the services and the insults of Condé, and to nominate to the rank of cardinal the same Gondi who had been the author of the barricades and forced the royal family to depart from the capital. When Turenne, in the mountains of the Ardennes, heard this news, he immediately endeavoured to carry out the terms of his treaty with Spain, by which a just and reasonable peace was to be afforded to the Spaniards. He wrote to Condé. A conference was opened at Stenay, which dragged on for two months, but had no result. Spain counted too much on the civil discords of France, and was not serious in the negotiation. Turenne, after two months, despaired of peace, considered reasonably that he had done all he possibly could, and returned to Paris 1st May, 1651.

From the depths of his exile Mazarin still influenced the regent. He saw the necessity of making terms with Turenne, and in virtue of a contract made in Paris, 20th March, 1651, the duchies of Evreux and of Chateau Thierry were granted to the Duke of Bouillon in exchange for the sovereignty of Sedan. The title of sovereign prince was granted to him as well as to Turenne, and Mazarin strongly recommended the queen to keep on good terms with Turenne and his brother.

Condé, with all his military talents, had not the capacity of retaining his friends. He was hardly restored to court before he began to disturb the new quiet. He sought for the government of Guyenne for himself, and for that of Provence for his brother Conti. These favours, probably through Mazarin's advice, were not granted by the regent. Condé threw himself into intrigue. Turenne refused to join his party. Condé rushed off to Montrond and declared openly against the court. The queen regent and the king moved to Bourges, and thence to Poictiers, where Mazarin joined them.

Mazarin, in December, 1651, returned to the court, which was at Poictiers, rather as a sovereign restored to

his dominions than as a minister driven from his post.
He was escorted by an army of 5,000 men, raised at his
own expense, or rather with the money of the nation
which he had appropriated to himself. The officers of this
force wore green scarves, the colours of the liveries of the
cardinal. Every party then had its scarf; white was the
colour of the king, and Isabel that of Condé. The queen
rejoiced at his return. The king, who had now attained
his majority, went to welcome him.

At the first news of his return, Gaston, alarmed, raised
troops in Paris. The parliament renewed its decree of
exile which proscribed Mazarin, and put a price on his
head, and the registers were solemnly searched to discover
what should be the price of the enemy of the kingdom.
It was found that in the time of Charles IX. a decree
promised 150,000 crowns to whoever should bring in
Admiral Coligny dead or alive. A similar decree was
passed, but nobody was tempted to deserve the reward,
which even if earned would not have been paid, and the
decree itself became nothing but a subject for ridicule.
Some wits placarded on the walls of Paris a supposititious
edict as to how the reward should be distributed; so much
was adjudged for cutting off the cardinal's nose, so much
for an ear, so much for an eye, and a larger sum for his
emasculation.

The ridicule with which this decree was received did not,
however, prevent another decree being passed, by which
his furniture and library were sold. The money was to be
devoted to paying an assassin, but it was, as was generally
the case, dissipated by the trustees.

The king (6th August, 1652), who had now attained his
majority, overturned the parliament of Paris and transferred it to Pontoise. Fourteen members who were attached

to the court obeyed, the others resisted, hence two parliaments arose, which to add to the confusion thundered
contrary decrees against one another.

A coolness had sprung up between Condé and Turenne
after the return of Mazarin.   Condé, resolved on civil war,
had gone to Bordeaux (22nd September, 1652), where he
had been received with enthusiasm; had treated with the
Spaniards, raised the south, and was prepared to carry war
to the Loire, with the intention of pressing the capital
with an army coming from the south and another army
coming from Champagne.

From this moment until the end of the civil war
Turenne was the leading man of France. The memoirs of
his young lieutenant, Duke of York, afterwards James II.,
confirm his own memoirs, and show that Turenne had
supported the court when it was terrified by Condé. The
retention of Turenne by Mazarin gave a guiding rein to
the government; securing the Duke of Bouillon was not
less important, since one had political genius and the other
military talent. The Duke of Bouillon entered the council
of the queen. The court moved to Tours and thence to
Blois, escorted by the troops brought by Mazarin. Nemours brought 6,000 men from Flanders, and joined
Gaston near Orleans, which declared for the nobles.
The court called in its troops from in front of Montrond
and from Champagne, and placed Turenne and Hocquincourt in command of them. By this means the court was
saved from an attempt to carry off the king by a detachment of the army of the princes by the personal gallantry
of Turenne, who seized the bridge of Jargeau (28th March,
1652), already half captured, and defended it bravely with
a handful of men notwithstanding the artillery fire of the
enemy.

The court then established itself at Gien, and Turenne and Hocquincourt, who commanded the royal army, occupied positions at Bleneau and Briare. The army of the princes on the Loire was commanded by the Dukes of Beaufort and Nemours. Neither of them had military talent. Their soldiers knew that Condé was 300 miles off, and in front of Turenne considered themselves lost, when in the middle of the night a single horseman appeared in the forest of Orleans in front of the outposts. The sentries recognized Condé himself, who had hurried from the Dordogne with the intention of reaching Paris. His presence restored confidence. He knew how much rapidity and boldness inspire courage. He had the talent of instantly making the boldest resolves, and of executing them with no less promptitude than ability. He quickly took Montargis. The royal army was separated, against the advice of Turenne, into two parts. Condé fell upon that which was at Bleneau (7th April, 1652), commanded by Hocquincourt, and this force was dispersed at the same time as it was attacked.

Turenne was not warned. Mazarin, terrified, fled to Gien in the middle of the night to awake the king. The court was in consternation. It was proposed to save the royal family by flight to Bourges. The victorious Condé was marching to Gien. Panic increased. Turenne by his coolness saved the court; marched direct against Condé with his own troops. He took a position where he could only be attacked with difficulty, and could not be outflanked, held Condé in check, and prevented him from pursuing his advantage. After several hours Condé fell back to Chatillon and Montargis, and Turenne to Briare.

Voltaire says it was difficult to decide which acquired the greatest honour, Condé by his victory, or Turenne who wrested from him the fruits of his victory. In this action at Bleneau, long celebrated in France, there were not 400 men killed, but Condé was on the point of seizing the whole royal family, and getting his enemy, Mazarin, into his hands. Such a small combat has seldom determined such great interests, or warded off a more imminent danger.

The prince could not hope to surprise Turenne as he had surprised Hocquincourt. He left his army and hurried to Paris, entered the capital, where, in the excitement of the moment, he seemed to be absolute master; but men's minds were divided. Parliament wavered between the court, the Duke of Orleans, and the princes. Every one declaimed against Mazarin; every one in secret was prepared to make terms with the cardinal to advance their own interests.

The court, through the successes of Turenne, moved by Auxerre, Lens and Melun, to Saint Germain, while Turenne covered its journey by threatening the enemy, and cut them off from Villeroy. The army of the Fronde, thus headed back, encamped at Etampes, which it fortified, on the direct road from Orleans to Paris. Turenne posted his army at Chartres, took many prisoners of the rebels who sought to go from Paris to the rebel army so as to protect the court, and watched the troops of the prince established around Etampes. Turenne wished the court, when at Melun, directly to enter Paris, where Condé was without troops; but Mazarin, fearful for his own sake, opposed the idea, and moved to Saint Germain. Turenne took all the avenues leading to Paris and drove back parties that sortied to the gates of the faubourgs, and occupied Saint Denis. He several times inflicted losses on the troops of the princes, carried the faubourg of

Etampes 5th May, 1652, and took 2,000 prisoners; as it was only the troops at Etampes which gave vigour to the party of the princes both in Paris and beyond the Loire. He then besieged Etampes (22nd May), and hoped to take it quickly, although the court could provide him neither with tools nor munitions sufficient, as he feared no relieving army, since the Spaniards were engaged in taking maritime towns on the frontier such as Gravelines, Mardyk and Dunkirk, and he trusted, by the dispersal of this force, to break up the only armed army which sustained the civil war. The princes, however, made a treaty with the Duke of Lorraine. He collected troops in Alsace and Flanders, and marched into France to raise the siege of Etampes. As soon as the siege was raised, the Lorrainers began to intrigue with the court. As he asserted at first that he was coming to serve the court, he obtained provisions everywhere on his road. His approach made Turenne more eager to take Etampes and disperse the troops of the princes before the arrival of the Lorrainers. The horses of the king and queen were used to draw artillery, and a battery was armed. His own regiment carried a ravelin with great gallantry; a lodgment was made, and the miner about to be attached to the walls when the Duke of Lorraine reached the Seine a little above Charenton. A bridge of boats was sent to him from Paris. Turenne could no longer remain before Etampes with an enemy in his rear, without lines of circumvallation or means of foraging. He was forced to raise the siege on 7th June. As the duke had always been trafficking with both sides since he left his country, no reliance could be placed on the greedy soldier of fortune. Mazarin indeed offered him more money to leave France than the Spaniards had given him to march in, and Charles IV. undertook to

retire. But Turenne took more effectual means than the
cardinal to insure his departure. Learning that the duke
was not intrenched he marched against him, threw himself
between the Lorrainers and the army from Etampes. In
vain Lorraine attempted to negotiate and gain time while
he threw up lines and completed redoubts. Turenne
would listen to no terms except the departure of the army
of Lorraine from France by a road chosen by himself.
The King of England, in the ranks of Lorraine, endeavoured
to negotiate with the Duke of York on the staff of Lorraine.
When the attack was imminent, Lorraine agreed to sign.
Turenne seized the bridge over the Seine; the treaty was
signed, and Lorraine gave hostages, and an hour after the
army of Lorraine began to move off towards the Rhine
Turenne took up a position under the walls of Paris
between the Seine and Marne. When the army of
Charles IV was actually leaving his immediate neighbourhood, the army of the princes appeared on the heights
on the further side of the river; but the Lorrainers
were under the cannon of Turenne, and they, though
willing to break their agreement, feared to do so. The
army of the princes moved away in the other direction, and established itself at Saint Cloud. A junction
between the princes and the Duke of Lorraine would
have driven the court to the last extremity. The royal
army moved from Villeneuve to Lagny and Dumartin, to
oppose a force from Flanders said to be moving down the
Oise. Condé seized Prissy to join this force. The court
came to Lagny, then to Saint Denis, and made a bridge at
Epinay to march against Condé at Saint Cloud. It was
reported that Condé was moving behind Montmartre to surprise the royal army. Turenne quickly moved and placed
his army at Saint Denis (2nd July). Turenne felt the

rear guard of the enemy, and drove him into the Faubourg St. Antoine. Condé wished his army to enter Paris, but the citizens refused him admission. Turenne followed his movements and harassed his rear guard. Strongly pursued, Condé was obliged to retire into the Faubourg St. Antoine, behind the intrenchments which the citizens had made to shelter themselves from the marauders of the Lorraine army, and which rested on one side on the hills of Charonne, and on the other on the Seine. Turenne attacked him, and thus was fought the celebrated battle of the Faubourg St. Antoine. Condé was on the point of being destroyed, for the city shut its gates, and he was pressed between the victorious troops of Turenne and the walls of the capital, when Mdlle. de Montpensier caused the guns of the Bastile to fire upon Turenne's army, and had the gate of St. Antoine opened for Condé. The civil war which might have been finished that day lasted in consequence for several years. Mdlle. de Montpensier was supposed to be anxious to marry the king, and Mazarin remarked that the discharge of the Bastile cannon had probably killed her husband.

The court which was still at Saint Denis, almost immediately found itself again in danger. An army of 200,000 Spaniards, joined by the Duke of Lorraine, soon invaded Picardy and marched on Paris. The court, having only an army of 8,000 men, contemplated flying to Lyons. Turenne opposed such a desperate course, which would have involved the loss of all the fortresses of Picardy, and given new flames to the civil war. He urged the occupation of the line of the Oise, which was agreed to. He placed the court at Pontoise, went with his troops to Compiègne to oppose the march of the Spanish army, and showed so bold a front that the archduke returned to Flanders, and

the Duke of Lorraine, with a Spanish auxiliary force, to
Champagne. While the court was at Pontoise, the Duke
of Bouillon, Turenne's brother and friend, died. Turenne
advanced against the Lorrainers. Mazarin left the court
10th August, and retired to Sedan. The Duke of Lorraine,
to join the army of the princes which was in Paris, again
(4th September) moved upon Paris to join Condé. Turenne
threw himself between them, but Condé joined the duke at
Ablin, taking up a position at Villeneuve St. Genor. For six
weeks Turenne rather hazardously remained in position in a
camp certainly not strong enough not to be forced, exposed
to the assault of a superior force; but Condé, failing in
his usual resolution and energy, did not attack, but
although superior by 3,000 men intrenched himself, hoping
to starve out the royal army. At last Turenne, through
want of forage, was forced to move (4th October), by a
retreat, during which Condé, again missing chances of
attacking, fell back to Senlis. Condé, in hopes of great
results from a junction with the Spaniards, marched
to meet them at Laon, whither the army of Lorraine
also fell back. Turenne then persuaded the court to
return to Paris. His advice was followed, and the result
proved that temerity is ever a better counseller than
timidity. The king entering Paris (21st October), was
received with joy by the population, and the Duke
of Orleans was forced to retire, and after some days
Cardinal de Retz was arrested. Shortly afterwards
(30th October), Turenne rejoined his army at Senlis,
moved forward, crossed the Meuse, forced Condé into
Luxembourg. Mazarin rejoined Turenne's army 17th
December, and began, against the prince and the Spaniards
a series of brilliant campaigns which brought on the treaty
of the Pyrenees. The Fronde was dead.

The court took advantage of the popular feeling in favour of order, reunited the parliaments of Paris and of Pontoise; but the assemblage of the chambers was forbidden. Parliament showed symptoms of remonstrance, but de˙ Retz was hurried into prison; some others were exiled, and parliament was silenced. Much was already changed. The absolute power of the Bourbons began to dawn.

CHAPTER VII.

MAZARIN, who had returned to Paris (3rd February, 1653), found himself in the presence of great difficulties. He had enemies both within and without the country. The Fronde was conquered in Paris, but not in the provinces. Guyenne was in revolt, and it was necessary to withdraw from the hands of suspected governors the strong places that they held.

During the internal troubles the fruits of the battles of Rocroi, Lens and Nordlingen had been lost (September, 1652). Dunkirk, Gravelines, and Mardyck had fallen into the hands of the Spaniards. Champagne was invaded. Rethel and Saint Menehould had been taken; Barcelona as well as Casale had fallen.

Lewis XIV. was in 1653 the absolute master of the kingdom, still reeling under the blows it had received, with an administration thoroughly disordered, with no ally except Savoy, but with no enemy except Spain, which was in a worse state than France herself, and whose best hope was in the presence of Condé in her ranks.

Mazarin did not despair of his country. He renewed his great designs of foreign policy, and determined to strike

heavy blows against the younger branch of the imperial
house. In Turenne he found his most skilful, most vigorous, and most devoted auxiliary. The cardinal was fortunate to have such an able captain, for the royal troops were
still much inferior to those of the Spaniards, although even
Condé was unable to restore to these the ancient glories
which he had wrested from them at Rocroi and Lens.
The Spanish army in Flanders mustered 20,000 infantry
and 14,000 horses. The Spaniards at La Capelle could
draw from Flanders supplies and munitions ; by way of
Stenay, which belonged to Condé, they communicated with
Luxembourg. From Rethel and Saint Menehould they could
forage to the very gates of Paris so long as Bordeaux resisted the government and diverted its aims. Turenne had
only 7,000 foot and 5,000 horses with which he had to
cover a large country and garrison several fortresses. He
had few stores and no artillery. If Condé could keep the
important strategical point of Rethel, having the Meuse on
his left, and Mouzon and Stenay, and the frontier of
Flanders on his right, whence he could draw provisions,
it became impossible to cover the whole country which he
threatened, which extended from Verdun and Vitry on one
side to Soissons and Guise on the other. The capture of
Rethel by Turenne would break into Condé's position and
separate his two lines of communication. Turenne saw
that as one of the enemy's corps was in Luxembourg,
the other on the Sambre, he might seize this place before
they had time to succour it. He quickly passed the Aisne,
and six miles beyond Rethel seized the point where the
two allied corps would have to join. Rethel was at once
invested. The garrison of 900 men was insufficient. The
attack was vigorously pushed. Outworks were carried, two
breaches made in the walls, and the town taken (9th July)

in three days, while the Spaniards were still considering which of their two corps should be moved to join the other. It was a great achievement. Condé could no longer begin the campaign on the Aisne. Hampered by Spanish counsellors, he had made a great mistake in not recognizing the importance of Rethel.

In return he urged the Spaniards at once to invade France, where Turenne had only 7,000 foot and 5,000 horses to bar their way, and most of the fortresses were without garrisons. The Spaniards entered Picardy between the Somme and the Oise.

Turenne could only manœuvre so as to hinder the movements of the enemy without being brought to battle, and prevent them from separating their troops to make sieges, or from pushing far into the kingdom through fear that their convoys would be cut off. He executed his plan with success. He ruined the great hopes which Condé had formed on the superiority of his troops by the rapidity and precision of his manœuvres. He disdained to waste his troops by garrisoning the fortresses. Constantly massing his army in the prince's neighbourhood, threatening him with battle, he as constantly avoided engagements by the excellent encampments which he chose, and prevented Condé from besieging towns by the fear of being himself immediately attacked. Rarely has the art of holding a skilful adversary in check by a system of temporisation been pushed so far.

In the autumn (1st September) the prince heard of the submission of Bordeaux. His principal object in pressing Paris was now defeated. He therefore marched on Rocroi, and invested it. Turenne could not attempt to raise the siege of Rocroi because his army was too weak, and the wooded and mountainous nature of the country afforded

the covering army great advantages.   He resolved to let
the place fall, and to compensate himself by taking
another.   He marched upon Mouzon, between Stenay and
Sedan, on the Meuse, which capitulated on the 28th
September.   The Duke of York, who was present at this
siege, was much impressed with the qualities of the French
generals, and especially with those of Turenne, of whom he
says that he saw everything for himself, and did not trust
to the reports of staff officers, as was the case with the
Spanish armies.   He in person marked out the trenches
and visited the works morning and evening.   It is to be
remarked that at this time Turenne had no engineers with
his army, and that the works had to be carried out under
the direction of the ordinary officers of infantry.

After the siege of Mouzon nothing important occurred
during the campaign. The fall of Bordeaux allowed the
court to bring up some troops from Guyenne.   With these
Saint Menehould was invested and taken on the 27th
November.   These successes finished the campaign of
1653, which was glorious for Turenne on account of his
bold marches, the skilful use that he frequently made of
field works, and the results which he obtained from his
sagacity by taking the three important places, Rethel, Saint
Menehould, and Mouzon ; while Condé, notwithstanding his
numerical superiority, had only been able to take Rocroi.

Turenne then. marched to cover Picardy, and a corps
under La Ferté watched the Duke of Lorraine on the
Meuse.   This year was also glorious for Mazarin, as he
restored complete order throughout the provinces as well
as in the capital of France.

The campaign of 1654 was only begun after the fêtes
of the consecration of the king which took place at Rheims
on the 7th June.   As Condé had assembled in Flanders

a considerable army which seemed intended for some great
enterprise, the war was almost personally directed against
him. It was determined to besiege Stenay, which belonged
to him, and which had long served as an asylum for the
Fronde. The direction of the siege was intrusted to
Fabert, the governor of Sedan. Turenne was meanwhile
to guard the frontier of Champagne, and to march there
to cover the besiegers, or towards Flanders, according as
the enemy attempted to raise a siege or to make an
approach towards Paris. Stenay was besieged on the 3rd
July. On the 6th Mazarin learnt that the Spaniards, in
place of endeavouring to raise the siege, had invaded
Artois, and begun to besiege Arras. If Arras fell, all the
acquisitions of France in Artois were threatened. A
powerful effort was necessary to save it. The governor
had only 4,000 infantry and 1,000 cavalry. Condé had
prepared the investment, which was so sudden that the
party of cavalry that had been sent out to reconnoitre
had been shut out. Turenne wished at once to march to
raise the siege, but received orders not to attempt to do so
until Stenay was taken and the troops besieging it could
be sent to his aid. On the fall of Stenay he found himself
at the head of 22,000 men, while Condé had had around
Arras about 30,000 ; but these by the fatigues of the siege
were reduced to equality with the royal army. The
Spaniards had made the mistake of opening trenches
against the strongest part of the fortifications, so that
after two months, during which they lost more than 3,000
men, they had only carried one ravelin. The governor
being attacked only on one point had not to divide his
garrison. He concentrated his troops on the side attacked
and disputed the ground foot by foot. Turenne on his side
caused the besiegers much suffering from want of provisions,

and he cut off their convoys from Douai and Saint Omer. One of these convoys met with a terrible catastrophe. While Turenne one night with the Duke of York was visiting the advance guards, they saw a sudden and violent light in the distance near Lens. The next day the cause of this light was explained. A whole regiment of Spanish cavalry marching from Douai, of which the officers and troopers were each carrying a sack of powder behind their saddles, as well as eighty horses carrying grenades, had all been burnt by the spontaneous discharge of the powder they were bearing.

The sound vigilance of Turenne caused the besiegers to want bread. On the other side Condé, seeing that many men were lost in his attack, and that the troops began to grumble, proposed to raise the siege. Turenne hoped by cutting off a convoy to compel him to do so, but having failed in this, and being informed by spies of the state of affairs, determined to attack, and went to reconnoitre the enemy's lines himself. He advanced so close that the horse of Lord German, who was with him, was killed, and some of his staff grumbled at being so much exposed. Turenne remarked that if he had been inspecting the part of the lines where Condé was such conduct would have been dangerous, but that in the Spanish service he knew that it would be necessary to warn the archduke, who would then summon Condé, take his counsel, and by the time that this had been done Turenne would have been safe back in his tent. At one in the morning of the 25th of July a general attack was made by Turenne on the lines of the besiegers. The Spaniards were driven off, and their camp seized. Their rout was complete. Condé alone remained with a disciplined army. He attempted an offensive return, which was happily stopped by Turenne.

Condé fell back, covering the retreat of the Spaniards,
collecting as he passed the troops who had remained in the
trenches.   He reached Cambrai, falling back from defile to
defile, and offering a front to the pursuing French.   He
saved thus a portion of the Spanish army, and obtained
from Philip IV. a well-deserved compliment when the king
said, "I know that all was lost, and that you have saved
all."   Condé had, however, not been able to save the
artillery, and the Spaniards left 4,000 men on the field,
3,000 prisoners, sixty-three guns, and all their baggage. It
was the fate of both Turenne and Condé to be beaten when
they commanded Spanish troops.   Turenne had with difficulty saved the relics of the army of Spain at Rethel,
when he was the lieutenant of a Spanish general.   Condé
had the same fortune before Arras.   Turenne received
much praise, and undoubtedly showed skill and vigour in
the field.   He was well supported in the cabinet by the
cardinal, who had shown indefatigable activity in furnish-
ing the army with men, provisions, and material.   That
these were supplied was due, however, greatly to the
representations of Turenne, and no campaign more than
this of 1654 shows us how constant he was in watching
over the supplies of munitions to his army, and the
improvement of equipment in the midst of the incessant
cares which the presence of Condé, the insufficiency of the
garrison of Arras, and the bad condition of his own troops,
gave him.   He kept up constant correspondence with
Le Tellier and Mazarin, pressing upon them all the details
of his situation, never complaining, but incessantly pointing
out what seemed to him necessary for the support of his
troops.   Our admiration for him must rise when we perceive how with the miserable resources he had at his hand
he did such great things.   His correspondence at this time

is a constant demand for carriage, provisions, staff officers, commissariat officers, tools, corn, bread, arms, pikes, and muskets, and reminds us strongly of the correspondence with the home government of the Duke of Wellington in the Peninsula. Notwithstanding the constant demands for these articles, which show their absence from the army, the troops were constantly moving and marching, convoys of the enemy were seized, spies taken, breaches stormed, the soldier everywhere faithful to his officer, the officer devoted to the soldier, both living miserably, but rushing with the same zeal to death or glory wherever the enemy threatened them, wherever it was necessary to risk life for king and fatherland.

It is said that Mazarin had thought that the raising of the siege of Arras would bring on peace, but if he truly thought so he was deceived. Voltaire asserts that Mazarin was absolute master of France and of the young king, as Don Lewis d'Haro was of Spain and Philip IV., and that they continued this war for their own glory ; but no one as yet heard the name of Lewis XIV., and no one ever spoke of the King of Spain. One crowned head alone in Europe had at that time any personal fame. This was Christina, Queen of Sweden. The Spanish government, awakened a little too late to the incapacity of their general, determined to confide to Condé the reorganization of their army and its supreme command, in order to make one last effort before the end of the campaign. Turenne did not allow time uselessly to pass away. Manœuvring between Cambrai and Bouchain, he crossed the Scheldt on the 6th September, seized Quesnoy, an important place, and thus curtailed much the Spanish quarters in Flanders. Quesnoy promised also to be a valuable base of operations for the campaign of the following year. The works were

strengthened, and Quesnoy put in a firm state of defence by the 1st November. Turenne pushed on towards Brussels, took Binch and Maubeuge, and then
rejoined the king at Guise. The raising of the siege of
Arras was a great success for the French army. Their
military prestige had been lowered by the civil wars. Its
political effect was also great, as at Paris there were intrigues going on to again raise the Fronde, and Cromwell,
it is believed, was only awaiting the taking of Arras to
break with France.

In the campaign of 1655 the French armies were concentrated at Guise on the 10th June. It was determined
to pursue the offensive and to besiege Landrecies, which,
with Quesnoy, opened the road into the Spanish low countries. Landrecies was invested on the 18th June. The
lines of circumvallation were complete in five days, and
the camp provided with provisions for a month. Condé,
who commanded the army of Flanders, took up position
between Guise and Landrecies, to cut off the provisions of
the besiegers and their communications with Paris. He
pillaged Picardy, but his efforts were useless. There was
already sufficient food in the camp. The outworks were
quickly carried ; Landrecies opened its gates (13th July)
after seventeen days of open trenches. The garrison
retired to Valenciennes, and the army of Condé fell back
on Cambrai (14th July).

The plan of the campaign was drawn up by Turenne in
this year in such a manner that the French army marched
down the Sambre as far as Bussiere, then, going back-
wards, moved through Avesnes and invested La Capelle,
which is one of the bulwarks of Picardy. To carry out
Turenne's resolution not to attack in front positions which
could be turned and caused to fall, it then retired upon

Bouchain, in order to pass the Scheldt below that town, leaving Valenciennes on the right, emerged on Condé, where it found itself by this movement in rear of the enemy's intrenchments near Valenciennes, which were turned. Turenne's advanced guard only just missed capturing Condé in person. If, indeed, the officer commanding had obeyed his orders, he would have done so, but he allowed himself to remain talking with some of Condé's officers because they were old acquaintances. He also deceived Turenne when he told him that Condé had been forced to escape by swimming the Scheldt. Turenne reported this to Mazarin in despatches, which were cut off and fell into Condé's hands, and a personal quarrel ensued between these two great captains, which was not arranged until the peace of the Pyrenees. On the 15th August Turenne invested Condé, and he so well guarded the approach of his convoys, and so vigorously pressed the attack, that the place capitulated on the 18th. On the 21st trenches were opened against St. Ghislain, a small fortress between Condé and Mons. The king and the cardinal were present at this siege, which was made difficult on account of the water which covered the country around. On the 26th the garrison surrendered, and the end of November the troops retired into winter quarters, after having occupied various camps for the purpose of consuming the forage which was found in their neighbourhood.

Towns had been taken, but peace did not appear nearer. The power of Condé and of his allies was little reduced. The garrisons which capitulated with the honours of war had the right of retaining their arms and rejoining the armies of their countrymen, and those that had not the honours of war accorded them lost their arms, which in a rich country such as the Low Countries could be again supplied during the winter. The victories of Turenne brought no definite result, except that his armies overran a certain amount of the enemy's territory—a result which indeed encouraged the troops and maintained their reputation abroad; but while forces were so evenly balanced decisive successes appeared still far off. New difficulties also were foreseen. Champagne had indeed been delivered from the foreign invader. The tide of invasion had turned, and French troops had poured into Hainault. There still remained the maritime towns of Gravelines, Mardyck, and Dunkirk to conquer. It was necessary to bring foreign auxiliaries to help.

Charles II., afterwards King of England, was then a fugitive in France with his mother and brother. A citizen had subjugated England, Scotland, and Ireland. Cromwell, a man well worthy to reign, had taken the style of Protector, and not that of king. He strengthened his power by the dignity with which he controlled it. He took heed of the privileges of which the English people were jealous. He did not billet soldiers in the city of London; he imposed no tax which caused discontent; he offended public sense by no show of pomp; he accumulated no private riches. His care was that justice should be observed with impartiality both by great and small. The brother of the ambassador of Portugal insulted some citizens in London and caused one to be assassinated. He considered that he would pass scathless because the person of his brother was sacred. He was wrong. Cromwell refused to pardon him, allowed him to be executed, and then signed a treaty with the ambassador. Never had commerce been so free in England or so flourishing, never had our country been so rich. Her victorious fleets made her name respected on every sea.

Mazarin, solely seeking to aggrandise and to enrich himself, allowed in France, justice, commerce, the mercantile marine, and finances, to languish. Master of France, as Cromwell was of England, after a civil war, he could have done for the country which he governed all that Cromwell had done for his. All the nations of Europe which had spurned alliance with England under James I. and Charles I. sought for it under the Protector. France and Spain, the two most powerful kingdoms in Christendom, intrigued against one another for the hand of fellowship from the country gentleman of Huntingdon. The Spanish ministry offered to aid Cromwell to take Calais. Mazarin proposed to him to besiege Dunkirk, and to hand over to England that town. Condé sought his aid, but Cromwell was too shrewd to negotiate with the prince who had little more behind him than his name—who had no party in France and no power in Spain. Cromwell's admirals had taken Jamaica to assure British commerce in the new world (May, 1665). After this expedition the Protector signed a treaty with the King of France on terms of equality. He forced the king to give him the title of brother. Cromwell's secretary signed before the plenipotentiary of France, and Cromwell forced the French government to expel from its states Charles II. and the Duke of York, grandchildren of Henry IV., to whom France gave an asylum.

It was only on the 23rd March, 1657, that an offensive and defensive alliance was signed between France and England, for during the year 1656 France had still to contest single-handed against Spain. The campaign that year began late, as negotiations for peace had been attempted at Madrid, and there were difficulties in obtaining money for the troops. The operations were directed against

three points—Valenciennes, Condé, and La Capelle. John
of Austria, the natural son of Philip IV. by an actress,
more worthy to command than the archduke, now commanded the army of Spain, aided by Condé. Turenne and
La Ferté commanded the French army, and determined to
invest Valenciennes, which was then one of the principal
Spanish towns in the Low Countries, but also one of the
most difficult to take. In it were situated all the magazines of Spain. It had a garrison of 1,600 soldiery, and
more than 10,000 inhabitants bore arms and served almost
as well as regular troops. A force of 20,000 men hovered
in the neighbourhood to impede the siege, and this force
was commanded by two great captains. The French had
not sufficient troops to include in their lines of circumvallation some heights which commanded their camp, and
which served as an observatory for the enemy. The
environs of the place were inundated, and the besieging
army was necessarily divided by the Scheldt into two
portions. Turenne took what precautions he could to
remedy the inconvenience of the situation. He had surrounded the two camps with a double intrenchment with
pallisades, constructed a dyke to stay the inundation,
thrown bridges across the Scheldt to assure the communications. The Spanish army, which was united at
Douai to raise the siege, attacked the lines of La Ferté
on the night between the 15th and 16th July, whilst a
false attack was made against Turenne. La Ferté was
routed and taken prisoner. Turenne met with a similar
reverse before Valenciennes to that which Condé had
before Arras. He saw nothing to be done but to raise the
siege. Turenne covered the retreat skilfully to Quesnoy,
where, although he had no tools to make intrenchments,
and although his officers wished to retreat further, he

stood firm, called together the remains of the army of La
Ferté, and sustained the morale of his troops. For this he
has been much praised by Napoleon, for he was the only
officer who had the courage to remain. If he had not done
.so a retreat would have demoralized the French army, and
probably rendered it unfit for any movements during the
remainder of the year.

The Spaniards took Condé. After Condé fell Turenne
passed the Scheldt to draw the war into Artois, and took
up a strong position between Lens and Arras. The Spanish
army did not venture an attack, but retired to invest St.
Ghislain. Turenne besieged La Capelle. The Spaniards raised
the siege of St. Ghislain to assist La Capelle, approached
within two miles of the lines of circumvallation thrown up
by Turenne, but did not care to attack them, and allowed
the place to be taken under_ their eyes on the 26th
September. The capture of La Capelle saved the honour
of the French army for the year, but did not compensate
for the check before Valenciennes. Mazarin pushed
forward more energetically his negotiations with the Protector, and on the 23rd March, 1657, the treaty of Paris
was signed. Its principal conditions were to bring on a
general peace ; that France and England should undertake
from the month of April at common cost and with common
forces the siege of Gravelines and Dunkirk by land and by
sea. After the conquest of these places Gravelines was to
belong to France and Dunkirk to England.

During a year from the time of the signature of the
treaty France and England engaged to conclude with
Spain neither truce nor treaty except by mutual consent.

At the end of May, 1657, 6,000 splendid infantry,
formed by Cromwell from respectable and well-paid men,
soldiers of the army of the new model, disembarked at

Calais to join the army of Lewis and serve in his pay. Before
their arrival the Spaniards had commenced operations by
throwing garrisons into Gravelines and Dunkirk and taking
St. Ghislain (22nd March).   In May Turenne took the
field and marched suddenly (28th May) on Cambrai,
which he invested.   He had not time to intrench himself
before Condé, who was at Valenciennes, advanced by forced
marches with his infantry against him, and at eleven on
the evening of the very day of the investment appeared in
front of the place with 4,000 horsemen, overthrew the
French cavalry, pushed into the place, formed his army in
order of battle on the counterscarp, and obliged Turenne
to raise the siege.   Turenne's design now was to besiege
some minor places in order to lead the Spaniards to withdraw a portion of the other garrisons from Dunkirk and
Gravelines, and then suddenly to take these towns.   La
Ferté laid siege to Montmedy (11th June to 4th August,
1657) and took it.

   Turenne held the Spaniards and Condé in check, and
used his English auxiliaries to protect Landrecies and
Quesnoy.   An attempt by the Spaniards on Calais failed
through the resistance of the place.   After the capitulation
of Montmedy Turenne quitted the Sambre, and in three
marches reached Saint Venant, whose position on the Lys
was very important.   So badly off was he now for money
that he was obliged to cut up his own plate and distribute
the morsels for pay amongst the English troops, who from
bad weather and want of money were suffering severely.
Animated by his generosity the soldiers pushed forward
the works with incredible diligence.   It was determined to
take the counterscarp, one of the most difficult operations of
the siege. The Puritan pikemen of Huntingdon and Hants
greeted with a loud shout of joy the order to advance,

rushed up the glacis, pushed through the palisade, swept over the covered way, and in full pursuit at the heels of the flying enemy went tumbling down the counterscarp, which twenty minutes before had been pronounced impregnable by the ablest of the marshals of France. This led to the fall of the place (29th August). Turenne then marched forward and forced the Spaniards to retire (15th September) under the guns of Dunkirk. They sent three Italian regiments to Mardyck, despatched several battalions to Gravelines, and encamped with the remainder of their army behind the canal of Dunkirk.

It was too late to besiege Dunkirk itself, but it was determined to attack Mardyck, which commanded the principal entrance to the Dunkirk canal from the sea, and the capture of which it was supposed would satisfy the English government, who did not cease to complain that their treaty for the capture of Dunkirk was not being carried out by France. Mardyck capitulated on the 3rd October, and this success established perfect harmony, which had been slightly disturbed between Mazarin and Cromwell. It was difficult to retain Mardyck through the winter. The army suffered grave inconveniences, as it could only encamp on the dykes. Desertion quickly began from the ranks, and even Turenne himself had to excuse it on account of the extreme necessity of the men. The troops had received no money since the beginning of the campaign. The cavalry had no bread; the English fell ill in great numbers. The enemy showed no signs of separating to winter quarters, and Turenne had to intrench himself, holding the great part of his troops together to cover the place. At one time so pressed was the army for necessaries that it was proposed to blow up the fortifications and abandon Mardyck. This roused the English Govern-

K

ment, and there arrived from London immediately palisades,
provisions, salt beef for the garrison, and necessaries for
the men. The soldiers plucked up heart. The enemy, informed of their relief, dispersed their army into cantonments in Flanders. During the winter Marshal d'Hocquincourt betrayed the French court and went to join
Condé in Flanders. The long war, famine in the provinces,
long-continued and heavy taxation, made people wish for
a change of ministry, without calculating whether the
change would be for the better or not.

Early in 1658 Turenne received orders from Mazarin,
who was much pressed on the point by Cromwell, to invest
Dunkirk. He moved by Cassel, crossed the Lys at Saint
Venant, passed the Colme near Beignes, and moved on
Dunkirk. The approach to the place was difficult, for the
inhabitants had opened sluices and the country was an
immense lake. The garrison consisted of 3,000 chosen men.

Condé and the Spaniards occupied Flanders with a
strong army, but dallied at Brussels, believing the siege of
Dunkirk impossible so long as the Spaniards held Beignes,
Furnes and Gravelines, and while still no forage could be
found in the country to feed the horses. There was no
wood for fascines or palisades near the town. Turenne
took a few outlying forts and then established his quarters
(May 25th) round the place, pitching his own camp on
the dunes on the side of Nieuport. He immediately
threw up lines of circumvallation and of contravallation,
which on the east and west rested on the sea. He assured the communications between the different parts
of his camp by bridges. He assured them between the
camp and Mardyck by having the road repaired by the
soldiers. He drew all his supplies from the sea, where
his base of operations was covered by the English fleet,

but found great difficulty in landing his stores. England furnished a fleet of eighteen vessels to prevent the town from being relieved by sea. The shore was guarded with booms and chains. Troops were pushed up from France, and the besieging army was fed from Calais by boats with provisions, forage, tools, palisades, and munitions, which could not be brought by land. Trenches were opened on the side of the dunes on the night of the 4th June. The works of intrenchment were finished when Turenne received new troops from France and 6,000 additional infantry from England, who formed a brigade under Morgan, an officer of high reputation.

The lines and bridges of communication being finished, on which ten days' work had been spent, the camp being provided with all necessaries for the subsistence of the troops, trenches were opened on the night between the 4th and 5th June; the siege progressed, constantly interrupted by sorties from the garrison—in which the English troops, who showed great courage but little skill in siege work, suffered seriously—and by attacks from detachments of the army of Condé, in one of which d'Hocquincourt was killed, and of Don Juan at Furnes. The news of the investment had surprised these generals at Brussels. They were determined to risk everything to save Dunkirk. They advanced, and pitched their camp on the dunes (13th June) about a mile and a half from the besiegers' lines, having with them 8,000 horse and 6,000 infantry. They had hoped to surprise Turenne in his lines, and had moved so hastily that they left their artillery behind. He determined not to remain passively to be attacked, but to march against them, leaving a strong guard in the trenches. On the 14th, at daybreak, he placed his army in order of battle. The left formed of the Lorrainers and English, rested on the sea;

the right rested on the canal of Furnes. The army was drawn up in three lines, and mustered 9,000 infantry and 6,000 cavalry. On each wing were five guns, and several frigates and sloops from the sea supported the attack, and annoyed the right of the Spaniards. These had taken up their position on the dunes—the right towards the sea commanded by Don Juan, the left on the canal of Furnes commanded by Condé. The infantry was in single line, the cavalry formed two lines on the right behind the infantry. The cavalry on the left was in six lines, the canals which intersected the ground making this curious division necessary. It was only at the last moment that Don Juan, notwithstanding the advice of Condé and the Duke of York, recognised that he was going to be attacked. He said to the Duke of York, "The French wished only to surprise the advance guard;" but Condé said to the Duke of Gloucester, who had never seen a battle, "In half an hour you will see how we shall lose one." The left wing of Turenne where the English fought charged with tremendous vigour against the right wing of the Spaniards. At the same time, as the tide went out, a dry place was left between the extreme Spanish right and the sea. Turenne immediately took advantage of the opportunity, pushed forward round the Spanish right, enveloped it, and showed for the first time his turning movements in battle, which he afterwards developed with great effect. Don Juan was completely defeated, and his right wing driven off the field. Condé, on the Spanish left, did everything possible to save it. Twice his impetuous charges forced the French squadrons to retire, but a battalion of French guards on the dunes pouring volleys into his right flank overthrew his squadrons. Condé's horse was killed under him, and he was nearly taken. The Spaniards had 1,000 men killed. Many of their soldiers were drowned in trying to save themselves, and 3,000 or 4,000 were taken prisoners. This battle, so prolific in result, was finished at midday. The army of Turenne returned to its lines. A sortie which the garrison attempted had been driven back by the guards of the trenches, but Turenne did not push his pursuit beyond Furnes because the great object of the French policy was now to take Dunkirk and give satisfaction to the English Government. Three days after the battle the regiment of Turenne effected a lodgment on the counterscarp. Still the governor steadily held out, but on the 23rd June he died of a wound, and the garrison, losing courage, demanded to capitulate. On the 25th it marched out of its fortifications as prisoners of war in the presence of Lewis XIV., who immediately occupied Dunkirk and handed it over to the English.

The delivery of Dunkirk to England was a bitter sacrifice for Lewis XIV., but Turenne compensated for it by numerous acquisitions in the neighbourhood.

Bergues was quickly taken. The Spanish army abandoned the field and occupied fortresses. Condé threw himself into Ostend, Don Juan into Bruges. Furnes fell 3rd July, Dixmude 6th July. A delay was now caused by a dangerous illness of Lewis, but Gravelines, invested on the 4th August, fell on the 27th, and Oudenarde forty-eight hours after. Turenne appeared before it 9th September. After the capture of Oudenarde it was expected that Turenne would march direct on Brussels. The Spaniards had indeed got some fresh troops together near Ypres. These could hardly have barred the way of his victorious army, but he preferred to move against Ypres and occupy the country between the Lys, the Scheldt, and the Dender.

With regard to the campaign Napoleon remarks that
Turenne committed the error, even after the battle before
Dunkirk, of not marching on Brussels, the seat of the
Spanish government in the Netherlands, and dictating
peace.   Political reasons may have prevented such a
course.

The moment Dunkirk was surrendered to the English,
Mazarin was assailed by public opinion in France, and was
accused of sacrificing the honour of his country and the
cause of his religion to a foreign and Protestant power.
It was advisable to besiege Gravelines without delay, since
the English, who were masters of the sea, were pledged to
assist in its capture, provided the siege took place not
later than September, 1659.

The march to Brussels would also have been tedious,
since it would have been necessary to take many towns on
the way to secure the line of communication.   The garrison
of Gravelines itself would have been a thorn in the side of
the advancing army.   Condé was still at the head of a
seasoned army.   A check might have been disastrous to
the whole policy of Mazarin at a time when the nobles
of Poitou, Anjou, and Normandy still meditated taking
up arms.   After the siege of Gravelines Turenne did send
detachments to within a few leagues of Brussels, but fell
back again for reasons which are not shown in his memoirs.
Possibly his army may have been weakened, and that he
found it necessary to consolidate the success which he had
already gained.   After the battle of Oudenarde he himself
explains that he did not march on Brussels, since, as he
had only one field train which could carry rations for only
three or four days, he could not besiege Brussels, and in
case of a check must have fallen back beyond Oudenarde,
to draw near his supplies from the sea.   Through rapid

marching he took Menin and its bridge over the Lys (17th September), and thus, after cutting in pieces a strong detachment of the enemy from Ypres, secured the communications between Dixmunde and Oudenarde. He then took Ypres (25th September), where the English gallantly carried the palisades in the counterscarp, which assured the communications to Oudenarde. He fortified these places, repelled all the attacks with which the Spaniards attempted to annóy his workmen, and Ypres, Menin, Oudenarde, and Dunkirk were strongly protected, and formed an almost impregnable quadrilateral in Flanders. Oudenarde was a most important point for future operations, as it lay at a distance of only four hours from Ghent and seven from Brussels. To prevent the enemy from annoying it during the winter he wasted the country around it as far as the Dender and to the gates of Tournay. He then withdrew his army into winter quarters, the English being sent to Amiens.

Constantly during this campaign Turenne kept up a correspondence with Le Tellier, advising the necessity of providing the troops with munitions, provisions, and pay, so that they might be able to move early in the spring. His correspondence everywhere shows a tenderness of feeling for the soldiery, which accounts for the manner in which he was loved by his men. Many generals have won the confidence of their troops, many generals have won the love of their soldiers, but few have combined respect and love in the ranks.

All was prepared to carry on a vigorous campaign in 1659, but war did not begin. Peace had been prepared by the victories of Turenne. On the 7th of May a truce of two months was agreed to. The preliminaries of a treaty of peace were signed in June, and on the 7th of November the peace of the Pyrenees was concluded. At the same time was made a contract of marriage between Lewis XIV. and the Infanta Maria Theresa. By this treaty France retained many of the places conquered, such as Arras, Lens, Gravelines, Landrecies, Thionville, Montmedy, Avesnes, Phillipville, in fact all the fortresses of Artois, and on the frontiers of Spain and Roussillon. The main point of the treaty for which Mazarin made many concessions was the marriage of Lewis XIV. with the Infanta, daughter of Philip IV. The treaty required that the princess should renounce her rights to the crown of Spain in a clause which gave occasion to much trouble afterwards.

The Duke of Lorraine retained his duchy, but was not allowed to maintain the capital as a fortified town, nor to have any troops.

Condé was restored to all his estates, honours, and dignities, but was made governor of Burgundy instead of Guyenne. By this peace, won through the victories of Turenne, a severe blow had been struck against the Spanish power, and a long stride taken towards French preponderance in Europe.

CHAPTER VIII.

TURENNE had never been in the habit, as was the custom of the time, of leaving his army the moment it went into winter quarters, and only returning when operations recommenced in the spring. Usually, for two or three months in the dead season, he went to Paris to consult the court, but he was absent from his troops much less than was usual with officers at that time in high command. Even after the long and glorious campaigns which led to the peace of the Pyrenees, he remained on the theatre of war to watch the defence of the fortresses, and to make arrangements for disbanding a portion of the army when peace was decided upon as well as to carry out the clauses of the treaty which related to the exchange of certain fortresses between the two governments. He received from Lewis a long memorandum with regard to the reduction of the army of Flanders, and with orders to put this difficult operation into immediate execution. He accomplished this duty with as much humanity to the soldiers as consideration to the officers, assuring to the first resources for a certain time, and arranging for the latter means of re-entering the army, or permission to take service in other countries.

He carried out slowly the disbandment of the troops, and more slowly still the return to the Spaniards of strong places occupied by the French. All was finished about the end of the year (1659). The troops of Condé were assured of pay and good garrisons, and were brought into the army of the king. On the 5th of April, 1660, he joined the king at Montpellier, and received as a reward for his campaigns the commission of Marshal-General of the armies of the king. Two days afterwards Turenne went with the court to Saint Jean de Luz, where the king's marriage with the Infanta took place. At the dinner which was held on the day of the ceremony, the King of Spain asked Anne of Austria if Turenne was among the great lords around the table, and when she pointed him out he looked at him, and then murmured in his sister's ear, "That is a man who has caused me many bad nights."

After this journey to the south, Turenne lived sometimes at Fontainebleau, sometimes at Paris—had relations with a great number of high persons in Europe, and had much to do with the diplomatic negotiations connected with the restoration of the Stuarts to the throne of England, before he had again to take the field against Spain.

On the 9th of March, 1661, Mazarin died. However much his financial administration may be blamed, it must always be remembered that the cardinal completed the policy of Henry IV., and Lewis XIII. raised the power of France abroad—concluded the peace of Westphalia, which gave France Alsace, Brisach and Philipsbourg, and the peace of the Pyrenees, which gave to her Artois, Roussillon, and a portion of Flanders.

The extraordinary compliment of court mourning was paid to Mazarin—an honour which was seldom bestowed on a subject, and had not been granted by the court of France since Henry IV. had ordered it for Gabrielle d'Estrées. He bequeathed to Lewis XIV. to continue his work and raise France to the first rank among nations, a brilliant circle of statesmen and soldiers—Colbert, Lionne, Condé, Le Tellier, Turenne—all united with one aim and with one object.

On the death of the cardinal, Lewis XIV. determined to have no future prime minister, but to govern himself. He followed out Mazarin's policy. He resolved to achieve the reduction of the Spanish branch of the house of Austria which had been begun by the treaty of the Pyrenees. This was the constant object of his foreign policy, and he laboured at it consistently from the year 1661.

Wiser than Mazarin, Lewis also devoted himself to the reorganization of all the branches of administration as well as of agriculture, commerce, industry, finance, the mercantile marine, and the army.

He began by establishing order in his finances, which had been deranged by a long course of peculation. Discipline was instituted among the troops. Magnificence, decorum, and grandeur embellished the court. The very pleasures of the king and his courtiers acquired brilliancy and greatness. All the arts were encouraged, and all employed to elevate the glory of the king and of France. Since the death of Henry the Great the French people had not seen a real sovereign. They had learned to detest the power of a prime minister, and were now filled with admiration and hope when they saw Lewis XIV. at twenty-two years old govern as Henry IV. had at fifty. The ancient factions quickly disappeared and left no trace behind. France soon became a monarchy, in which there was but one master and many subjects.

Lewis quickly showed that he determined not only to be

absolute at home but respected abroad. At this time the
Emperor of Germany was considered superior to all sovereigns, and the German chancellery did not accord to other
kings the title of majesty. The sovereigns of France
claimed the title of Very Christian. The kings of Spain
opposed it with the title of Catholic. Constant intrigues
between these two powers went on at Rome for precedence
in ceremonies and on state occasions. The dispute had
never been decided. A pace or two further forward in a
procession, a chair placed near the altar or opposite the
pulpit of a preacher, were, at Rome, the triumphs of rival
diplomatists, and established titles to pre-eminence (1661).
It happened that when a Swedish ambassador was entering
London, Count d'Estrade, the French ambassador, and
Baron de Vatteville, ambassador of Spain, disputed for a
front place. The Spaniards had the horses of the French
carriages killed, and the suite of D'Estrade was wounded
or dispersed. Lewis, informed of this insult, recalled his
ambassador from Madrid, sent the Spanish ambassador
from France, and caused Philip IV., his father-in-law, to
be told that if he did not recognise the superiority of the
crown of France, and make compensation for the affront,
war would begin. Philip was in no condition to plunge
his kingdom again into war for the sake of the precedence
of an ambassador. He sent an envoy to Lewis at Fontainebleau, who, in presence of all the foreign ministers
in France, declared that Spanish ambassadors would no
more compete with those of France (24th March, 1662).

The Duke of Crequi, French ambassador at the Vatican,
disgusted the Romans with his pride, while his servants
committed in Rome the same disorders as the undisciplined
youth of Paris, who then considered it an honour to attack
every night the watchmen of the town. Some of Crequi's

lackeys charged, sword in hand, a squad of Corsican guards
of the pope. The whole regiment insulted came in arms to
besiege the house of the ambassador (20th August, 1662).
They fired on the carriage of Madame Crequi, killed a
page, and wounded several servants. The duke left Rome,
accusing the relations of the pope and the pope himself of
having favoured this outrage. The pope was struck with
consternation when he heard that Lewis actually threatened to besiege Rome, that French troops were already
passing into Italy, and that the affair had become a quarrel
between the nations. In vain the Holy See sought the
mediation of all the Catholic princes. Circumstances
were not favourable. The empire was attacked by the
Turks, and Spain was embarrassed with an unfortunate
war against Portugal.

In France the parliament of Provence summoned the
pope to appear before it for permitting an outrage on its
sovereign, and seized the county of Avignon, an appanage
of the Holy See. In the Middle Ages excommunication
would have been the reply from Rome, but this had now
become an antiquated and obsolete weapon. The pope had
to yield to exile from Rome his own brother, who had been
connected with the assault on the French embassy, and to
send a legate to give satisfaction to the king, to disband
the Corsican guard, and to raise in Rome a pyramid with
an inscription which told the tale of the injury and its
reparation. Cardinal Chigi, the legate on this occasion,
was the first envoy from the court of Rome who had
ever been sent to ask for pardon. Former legates had
ever come to give laws or to impose decrees. Lewis
granted peace, but required some more solid satisfaction
than an inscription, for he forced Rome to yield up Castro
and Ronciglione to the Duke of Parma, and to compensate

the Duke of Modena for Commachio, and thus acquired
the solid honour of being regarded as the protector of the
lay princes of Italy.

Lewis in supporting his dignity did not neglect to
increase his power. His finances were so well managed by
Colbert (1662) that already he enjoyed a far larger
revenue than at the death of Mazarin, and he found himself in a position to purchase Dunkirk and Mardyck from
the needy King of England for five million pounds
(27th October, 1662).

Charles II., prodigal and poor, felt no shame in selling
the prize of English blood. Hyde, his chancellor, for
having supported his sovereign's crime was banished from
England by a parliament which seldom fears to punish
the faults of favourites, and, when necessary, even to judge
kings themselves. Lewis immediately hired 30,000 men
to work on new fortifications at Dunkirk and to dig a
basin capable of holding thirty ships of war, so that hardly
had the English sold this town than it became an object of
alarm to them (30th August, 1662). Shortly afterwards
the Duke of Lorraine was forced to give up the strong
town of Marsal, and the unfortunate Charles IV., a
tolerably skilful captain, but a feeble, inconstant, and
imprudent prince, had to make a treaty by which he gave
Lorraine to France after his death.

The Turks were then formidable in Europe. They were
attacking at the same time the Emperor of Germany and
the Venetians. The policy of France had been since the
time of Francis I. to be allied with the Turks, not only for
the advantage of commerce but to prevent the house of
Austria from becoming too powerful. Still, a Christian
king could hardly refuse succour to the emperor when in
too great danger, and it was the policy of France that

although the Turks should annoy Hungary they should
not invade it. Lewis made a treaty with the emperor,
sent 6,000 men into Hungary officered by the choicest of
the nobility of France. These French troops served in
Hungary under Montecuculli, who, afterwards serving
against France, was a formidable opponent of Turenne.
There was a great battle at St. Gothard on the banks of
the Raab between the Turks and the Christian armies
where the French contingents showed great gallantry.
Lewis, while openly aiding the emperor, secretly supported
Portugal against Spain. Mazarin had abandoned the
Portuguese by the treaty of the Pyrenees, but Spain had
made some tacit infractions of the peace—France made
one more palpable. Marshal Schonberg, a foreigner and
Huguenot, passed into Portugal with 4,000 French soldiers,
whom he paid with the money of Lewis, but pretended to
pay with that of Portugal. Schonberg's troops joined the
Portuguese, and gained a complete victory at Villa Viciosa,
which assured the Portuguese crown to the house of
Braganza (17th June, 1662).

Thus Europe looked upon Lewis already as a warlike
prince before even he ever made war.

He was allied with Holland (1667) when this Republic began war with England, nominally on account
of the empty honour of the flag — really for the sake
of commerce in the Indies. Lewis saw with pleasure
the two maritime powers each year placing on the
seas against each other fleets of more than one hundred
vessels, and mutually destroying themselves by the most
obstinate naval battles that had ever been fought
(1667). Lewis endeavoured to establish a navy, but
while the English and Dutch covered the ocean with
nearly 300 large ships of war he had still only fifteen or six-

teen which were employed against the pirates of Barbary,
and when the States-General pressed him to join his fleet
to theirs there was at Brest but one fire boat. This disgrace Lewis earnestly set himself to remove so well that in
1667 he had a navy of 110 ships of different sizes. Meanwhile the land army had been, under the skilful guidance of
Turenne, greatly improved and augmented, and was now
in a magnificent state. Notwithstanding the disbandments
which followed the peace of the Pyrenees Lewis had still
under arms about 125,000 men, drilled and disciplined in a
manner which had never yet been seen in an European army.
His troops had learnt the art of war. His officers had been
trained in Hungary, Holland, Portugal, and other foreign
fields, as were later those of England, till weak ministers
framed a foreign enlistment act and deprived our army of
one of the most valuable modes of education for its business.
There was no power which he had to fear. England was
devastated by pestilence, London reduced to ashes by fire.
The prodigality and continued indigence of Charles as
dangerous to his country as plague and fire, made France
perfectly safe on the side of the English. The emperor
was recovering slowly from the exhaustion of the Turkish
war. Philip IV. dying, left a monarchy as feeble as himself. Lewis was the sole important sovereign in Europe.
He was young, rich, well served, blindly obeyed, and
sought with impatience to distinguish himself and to
conquer.

The opportunity soon presented itself. Philip IV., his
father-in-law, had by his first wife, sister of Lewis XIII.,
the Princess Maria Theresa, now married to Lewis XIV.
Through this marriage the Spanish monarchy at last came to
the house of Bourbon, which had been so long its enemy.
Philip by his second marriage, with Maria Anne of

Austria, had Charles II., a sickly infant, who alone re-mained of three sons, of whom two died in infancy. Lewis raised a claim on the death of Philip that Flanders, Brabant, and Franche Comté, provinces of Spain, should, according to the law of these provinces, revert to the Queen of France, notwithstanding that she had renounced her rights to the crown of Spain. If the claims of nations could be judged by an impartial tribunal, as are those of individuals, the question would have led to much special pleading. Lewis caused his claims to be examined by his councillors and theologians, who not unnaturally declared them to be incontestable, but the councillors and con-fessors of the widow of Philip IV. found them, just as natu-rally, untenable. One of the pretexts that the council of ·Lewis raised was that the dowry guaranteed by Spain to Maria Theresa had not been paid. It was forgotten that the dowry of the daughter of Henry IV. also had not been paid. A. long correspondence ensued. The neutrality of Leopold of Austria was secured by a special treaty, and Lewis, trusting more to the sword of Turenne than the representations of his ambassadors, marched into Flanders to assured conquests (1667).

Lewis himself was at the head of the army, but Turenne was the directing genius, and was the true minister of war, for Le Tellier, the nominal minister, acted under his orders. It was Turenne's eye that inspected the men, their equipment, their arms, watched them manœuvre and defile with the attentive and severe glance of a great captain accustomed to the thousand details of military life, which is of much more importance for the well-being of troops than the majestic and distracted gaze of a young prince less occupied in seeing well than in being seen well. The Marquis Castel Rodrigo was the Spanish governor in

L

the Low Countries. He was a man of spirit and of bravery,
but the provinces were almost without defence, for he
could not supply finances which had been exhausted by
the peculations of his predecessor, nor could he atone for
the weakness and slowness of the council of Madrid.
Careless of his own interests and his own fortune, he
showed extraordinary zeal for those of his sovereign, but
he was no soldier. He had reached the age of forty-five
without ever having seen a battle, or gained a practical
insight into war—a science so difficult that theory alone
never can teach it. He had forbidden the clothes and the
colours and the fashions of St. Germain, and desired that
the court of Spain should be the model imitated at
Brussels. He found it impossible to change old customs
which the vicinity of Paris contributed to keep up, and
which the Spaniards in the Low Countries had themselves
accepted. He only succeeded in dissatisfying everybody.

The strong places in Picardy having been furnished
with provisions and munitions of war, and 50,000 men
having been discreetly placed along the line of the Sonne,
chosen from the best troops of France, early in May
Turenne took the command, and placed himself at the
head of a most formidable army. On the 16th of May the
king left St. Germain. He was about to study war under
the greatest and most perfect of its masters. Louvois,
just made minister of war, came also to perfect himself in
the science of administration. Before the king joined the
army Turenne had taken Armontières and Binche. Lewis,
when he joined Turenne, was at the head of 35,000 men
as a corps ready for battle. Another corps of 8,000 was
sent towards Dunkirk in observation, and to move by the
sea ; one of 4,000 towards Luxembourg, to cover the right
flank. Colbert had multiplied the financial resources of

the state to furnish the necessary expenses; Louvois was making immense preparations for the campaign; magazines of all kinds were established on the frontier. He first introduced the system, which the weakness of the government had hitherto made impracticable, of allowing armies to live by magazines. Whatever siege the king wished to undertake, to whichever side he wished to turn his armies, supplies of every kind were ready, billets for the troops marked out, and marches laid down. Discipline, made more severe every day, held the officers to their duty. The presence of the young king, the idol of his army, made duty easy and light. Military rank from that time began to be an honour above the rank of birth. Services, and not ancestry, were now regarded as honourable. Thus an officer of the lowest birth was encouraged, while those of the highest had no cause to complain. The infantry, on whom now fell the weight of war, since the uselessness of lances had been recognised and fire improved, partook the rewards which hitherto had been bestowed on cavalry alone, although still half of an army was composed of mounted men, and infantry were still formed in four ranks, the fourth being armed with the .pike, till Vauban finally suppressed pikes, and made foot-soldiers rely upon their fire. Nor was then this formation unreasonable, since artillery was still in small proportion, there being only about three guns to 2,000 men. The king of France, with all these advantages, was moving into the defenceless provinces of a ruined and decaying kingdom. He had only to do with his mother-in-law, a weak woman, ruled by a Jesuit, whose despised and unfortunate administration left the Spanish monarchy without defence. The art of attacking fortresses was still little understood, and that of defending them was still more faulty. Ignorance, poverty, and carelessness left the frontier of Flanders almost without defence. Lewis marched into Charleroi as if it had been Paris. Turenne, struck with its position between Mons and Namur, counselled the king to restore its defences, and to halt there the necessary time. The whole army worked there for fifteen days under the direction of Vauban, and marched again on the 16th June, having left in Charleroi a garrison of 2,400 men.

Turenne, whose advance on the Sambre was merely to deceive the Spaniards as to his true intentions, fell back on the Scheldt, passed between Mons and Brussels, and marched on Ath. Ath, Tournai, Furnes, and Courtray quickly fell. Trenches were opened against Douai, which was carried in a few days (6th July, 1667). Oudenarde was taken. Dendremonde was saved from surprise merely by the waters of inundation. Lille, the most opulent city of the Low Countries, and the only one well fortified, which held a garrison of 6,000 men, capitulated after seventeen days of siege, of which the works were directed by Vauban (27th August). The siege of Lille shows a great improvement on the mode in which sieges had hitherto been conducted. On the 10th the place was invested and a line of contra-vallation thrown up to prevent sorties on the garrison. The next day a line of circumvallation protected the camp against the attacks from without. On the 18th the trenches were opened; on the 19th a battery of twenty-five guns was armed; on the 21st the artillery began to batter the place; on the night of the 22nd the trenches were pushed to the glacis, and at midnight of the 25th the French guards and the regiments of Picardy and Orleans attacked the covered way and carried it. A battery was immediately constructed on the counterscarp, armed with twenty-two guns, and began to breach two of the ravelins ; these were carried on the night of the 26th by the musketeers and the French guards. The capture of the ravelins allowed the assault of the *enceinte*, but before it was made the garrison, reduced to 2,400 men, capitulated.

Marsin, with 8,000 troops, which composed the Spanish army, advanced towards Lille before it fell. Turenne, immediately after the capitulation, quickly made his dispositions to cut off the Spanish retreat, and though this did not succeed he cut their rear guard to pieces, and took from them 1,500 prisoners, their standards, and their drums (31st August). The remainder of their troops sought refuge in Brussels or Mons.

In September the king returned to Paris, leaving Turenne in command of the army. The Spaniards formed the intention of starving his troops during the winter, and began fortifying Alost. Turenne attacked the town suddenly without works of approach, and the fortifications were destroyed at the end of September. The troops had, however, suffered much from hunger and fatigue ; many were sick, many had to be used as garrisons of the taken places. The weather was exceedingly wet and the army suffered much. Impotent to defend its states, the Cabinet of Madrid appealed to all the jealousies which could be excited against France, and strove to raise Holland. The Dutch, who by no means desired the French as their neighbours, interfered in favour of Spain. In July they pressed Lewis to explain clearly his intention. They renewed their demands after the taking of Alost. The campaign of 1667 was conducted very differently from those of previous wars. Turenne for a long time had nothing but iron plates in his camp. It was only at the siege of Arras, in 1657, Humiers used silver plate, and

had roasts and sweets, but in this campaign, where the
young king, loving magnificence, brought the brilliancy of
his court into war, everybody revelled in taste, clothes,
and equipages. Luxury, the sure sign of the wealth of a
state, and often the cause of its fall, was abundant, yet
bravery was everywhere manifest. Fatigue was despised.
Officers went into the trenches with helmets on head and
cuirasses on back. The king gave the example. He
visited the trenches in front of Douai and in front of
Lille. As soon as the campaign was over the towns taken
were fortified. Vauban, one of those great men of genius who
appeared for the service of Lewis, was entrusted with the
fortifications. He constructed them according to his new
method. Men were surprised to see places no longer
surrounded by high walls and frowning battlements, but
merely by works almost level with the ground. The high
fortifications which had hitherto been raised were exposed
to be battered down by artillery. The lower they were
made the less were they in danger. The citadel of Lille was
constructed on these principles (1668). Never yet had the
civil government of a town been separated from that of
the fortress; the first example was at Lille, and Vauban
was the first governor of the citadel.

The Dutch, fearing more and more to see the French
reappear in Flanders, approached England and Sweden, and
opened negotiations for a triple alliance. It was arranged
and signed in five days (23rd January, 1668), but French
diplomacy was then wonderfully managed. Lionne had able
agents, and all the views that had been exchanged between
Amsterdam, London, and Stockholm were regularly known
at Paris. Warned of the negotiations of the Dutch, Lewis
resolved to anticipate them. Then arose a conspiracy
against Turenne, which for nine years exercised an influ-

ence on all warlike matters in France. It was he who
had arranged with the king the plans of the campaign.
It was he who had organised the preparations and directed
their execution, and when the troops were taking up their
winter quarters it was to him still that Louvois should
have rendered account of measures taken or to be taken.
Turenne, however, never flattered Louvois, and always
preserved towards him the dignity of a superior. Under
the able and severe tuition of Turenne the young Secretary
of State for War had made rapid progress, but now that
he knew his strength, had gained experience, and felt
fortune smile upon him, he writhed under the yoke. His
father helped him to undermine the influence of Turenne.
He believed that he would diminish the power of Turenne
in giving him a rival, and he insinuated to the king that
the genius of the marshal, great as it was, would not
suffice for all the developments of war, that for the execution of his great projects he had need of more than one
lieutenant, and that it would be both a magnanimous and
useful act if he employed the military talents of Condé.
The king was easily convinced—Condé was taken back
into favour, and to his honour it must be said that Lewis
had never to reproach himself for giving him his confidence. The king gave him full and entire trust from
the first day of the reconciliation; informed him of the
intrigues of the Dutch, and of the designs which he had
to destroy their calculations by a sudden attack on Franche
Comté (1668). The court at St. Germain was dallying
with amusement, when, in the middle of winter in January,
men were astonished by seeing troops moving on all sides.
Trains of artillery, parties of munitions, were moving for
various reasons along the roads which led from Champagne

into Burgundy. That part of France was busy with
movement. Foreigners through interest, courtiers through
curiosity, were lost in conjectures. Germany was alarmed.
The object of these preparations and of these marches was
unknown to all. On the 2nd February the king started
from St. Germain with some courtiers; Condé was already
with the troops. The day that Lewis arrived at Dijon
20,000 men, assembled by different roads, were in Franche
Comté, at some miles from Besançon. Besançon was
quickly taken. Dôle fell (14th February, 1668) twelve
days after the king left St. Germain, and in less than
three weeks all Franche Comté submitted to Lewis. This
conquest, more rapid even than that of Flanders, produced admiration in France, indignation abroad. The
Dutch renewed their remonstrances. Lewis was determined vigorously to push the war in the Low Country, and
more than 100,000 men were concentrated on the frontier,
but the triple alliance officially known divided the court.
Turenne, Condé, Louvois counselled the king to break this
barrier and push forward. Colbert and Lionne, who held
that France had not the arms, money, nor alliance to
support a general war, were of contrary opinion. Lewis
was indignant that a tiny state such as Holland should
conceive the idea of barring his conquest and of being the
arbiter of kings; still more indignant was he that Holland
was able to do so. He meditated vengeance, but at present he would not risk a European coalition. A phantom
congress was assembled at Aix-la-Chapelle under the
nominal supremacy of the Pope. The real negotiations
were carried on at St. Germain, and when all was agreed
were sent to Aix-la-Chapelle to be signed (15th April,
1668).

By this treaty Lewis gave up Franche Comté, but retained a portion of his conquests in Flanders. He did not forget this insult on the part of the Dutch, and by the fortresses which he had gained in Flanders he made a way towards Holland of which at some time he determined to avail himself.

CHAPTER IX.

WAR IN HOLLAND.

AFTER the peace of Aix-la-Chapelle Turenne devoted the time which peace allowed him to the religious studies that he had begun some years before, and became a convert to Catholicism. Lewis XIV. actively prepared to ruin the people who had arrested him in the midst of his successes. He continued to regulate his resources, to fortify and embellish his kingdom. It was seen that an absolute king who wishes success could obtain it almost without trouble. He had only to command, and adminis-trative successes were as rapid as had been his conquests. The seaports, formerly ruined and deserted, were now surrounded with works which defended and adorned them. The seas were covered with vessels and sailors, and the navy now counted sixty great vessels of war. New colonies, protected by his flag, were established in America, in the East Indies, and on the coast of Africa. In France immense buildings occupied the labour of thousands of men, and nearer the court and capital more ingenious arts gave France comforts and civilisation of which pre-ceding centuries had no idea. Letters flourished, good taste and sound reason arose.

Lewis, little heeding the capture of Candia by the Turks, devoted all his attention to his great design of conquering the Low Countries, and determined to begin with Holland. The Dutch, proud of the result of their intervention in favour of Spain, had caused a medal to be struck, in which they represented themselves as the defenders and conciliators of kings, the avengers of the liberties of the seas, and the preservers of the peace of Europe. This was a great blow to the vanity of Lewis, which he never forgot. He was advised by Condé that the true means to conquer the Low Countries was to reduce the Dutch, and, if possible, annihilate them. He wished also to crush the Dutch power in the Indies, and to give to the French colonies in Asia and to the French navy the rank and preponderance of the united provinces. The opportunity became every day more favourable. The republic ruled the sea, but on land was very weak. Allied with Spain, and England at peace, it rested too securely on treaties and on the advantages of an immense commerce. Its land army was as ill provided and despicable as was its navy disciplined, invincible, and respectable. Its cavalry was composed only of burghers, who never left their homes, and who paid substitutes for the scum of the people to do duty in their place. The infantry was almost on a similar footing. The officers, even the commandants of fortresses, were the sons or relations of burgomasters, brought up in ignorance and idleness. John de Witt, the pensionary, had a wish to correct these abuses, but he had not been sufficiently earnest.

Lewis made no overt act of hostility until sufficient time had been allowed for a thorough organisation of both his navy and army. The first anxiety then was to dissolve the triple alliance and gain England. It was not difficult

for Lewis to secure Charles. The English king had not
been very sensible to the shame which his crown and his
nation had suffered when his vessels were burnt in the
Thames by the Dutch fleet. He thirsted neither for revenge or conquest; desired to live in his pleasures, and
to reign without being troubled by a parliament. Lewis
promised money to Charles, which would enable him to
dispense with legitimate supplies. This secret understanding between the two kings was trusted in France only to
Madame, sister of Charles II., wife of Monsieur, the only
brother of the king, to Turenne, and to Louvois. This
princess was the plenipotentiary who carried out the
treaty. She met her brother at Canterbury. Charles,
moved by the money of France, signed all that Lewis
wished, and the spoils of the Dutch were divided in an-
ticipation between the courts of France and England.

Rumours of this understanding gradually spread abroad,
but Europe heard them in silence. The emperor, occupied
with seditions in Hungary; Sweden, kept in play by negotiations; Spain, always feeble, irresolute, and slow—all left
a free career to the ambition of Lewis. The Elector of
Bavaria promised not to enter into the alliance. The
Elector of Cologne undertook to give the French a passage
through his country, provisions, and magazines, and to
let them build a bridge over the Rhine. The Bishop of
Munster opened his states and placed his resources at the
disposal of the king for a monthly subsidy. The Bishop
of Osnabrück agreed to allow French armies to move
through his territory. The Dutch found themselves without any allies except the Elector of Brandenbourg and
Spain, and from these only obtained uncertain promises.
Colbert, by his able administration, was in a position
to provide for all the expense. Louvois put at Lewis's

disposition the most formidable means of attack. Levies of men were made in England, Italy, and Switzerland. All French officers serving abroad were recalled. Bridges were made in the arsenals in small pieces for crossing the rivers. 40,000 cavalry were raised, and a large number of infantry. Five arsenals were built and fortified, at Brest, Rochefort, Toulon, Dunkirk, and Havre. An army of marines was ready, for the seaport populations had been for some years enrolled in the maritime inscription; and 35,000 mariners were ready for the fleet, which consisted of 120 ships, armed with 5,000 guns. The land army mustered 172,000 men; the field artillery consisted of ninety-seven guns; there were ready three field equipages; transport trains were provided to carry 260,000 rations.

Holland, to add to its dangers, was divided into two factions—one of rigid republicans, to whom every appearance of despotic authority seemed a monstrous outrage on the laws of humanity; the other of moderate republicans, who wished to restore to the position held by his ancestor the young Prince of Orange, afterwards so well known as William III. The grand pensionary, John de Witt, and his brother were at the head of the austere partisans of liberty; but the party of the prince was gaining power.

All that ambition and human prudence could effect was prepared to destroy Holland. There are few examples in history of an enterprise undertaken with such formidable preparations. Few invasions against so weak an enemy have been begun with so many regular troops and so much money as Lewis employed to subjugate a dominion not much larger than the principality of Wales. The English fleet was to join with the French. The generals of the army, under the king, were Condé and Turenne; Luxem-

bourg commanded under them ; Vauban was to conduct the
sieges ; Louvois was present to watch over all with his
usual vigilance.

Never as yet had an army so well disciplined and so
magnificent been seen on the fields of Flanders. The
household brigade had been newly re-formed. To it were
attached four companies of guards, composed each of 300
gentlemen, amongst whom were many young cadets without pay, 200 gendarmes of the court, 200 light cavalry,
500 musketeers—all gentlemen chosen for their youth and
their soldierlike qualities ; 100 Swiss, the very body-guard
of the person, accompanied the king, and mounted guard
before his billet or in front of his tent. These troops,
glittering with gold and silver, were an object of terror
and admiration to the country people, among whom magnificence was unknown. Discipline, becoming constantly
more exact, had given greater facility of manœuvre and
greater precision of movement to the army. There were
not as yet inspecting generals, but two men, each renowned, performed these functions. Martinet, whose
name has descended as a disciplinarian, superintended
the discipline of the infantry, and had a year before
introduced the bayonet in some regiments instead of the
pike, and for the first time a correspondent accompanied an
army to record its prowess, for the king took with him an
historian, who was to write the tale of his victories. Nor
was this all. Louvois had secretly bought a large part
of the munitions which the Dutch were collecting, and
thus deplenished their magazines.

Against Turenne, Condé, Luxembourg, Vauban, 130,000
combatants, an enormous artillery, and much money,
Holland could only oppose a young prince of weakly constitution, who had seen neither sieges nor campaigns, and

about 25,000 land soldiers. William of Orange, twenty-two years old, had just been elected captain-general of the forces by the wish of the people. The grand pensionary had consented. The Dutch chose the line of the Yssel as their principal barrier against invasion. It was not sufficient to secure their territories, since it rested on two weak places, Schenck and Nimeguen. If these fell the line of the Yssel was easily forced, and as there was no second line of defence to stop the enemy the united provinces were uncovered. De Witt proposed an offensive policy. He urged the States-General to fall with all the force of the republic on the towns near the Rhine, where the French had established magazines to destroy them, push into the territories of Cologne and the bishopric of Munster, and disperse the troops of France. This expedition might have been successful, for it would have carried the war away from Dutch territory and given time to rouse against France the jealousy of Germany and Spain; but consultative bodies never adopt a vigorous policy, and the States, under the pretext that war was not declared, prevented the troops from assuming the offensive, and made them remain in defensive positions where the obstacles to their success were almost insurmountable. Then France and England declared war against Holland, the Elector of Cologne and Bishop of Munster soon imitated the two crowns, and the campaign of 1672 began.

CHAPTER X.

IT was determined that the campaign on the French side should be conducted by three armies, and with a siege train and a transport train, which marks a new era in the art of war. One of these armies of 40,000 men, under the immediate orders of the king, was commanded by the Duke of Orleans, his brother, as generalissimo, with Turenne as marshal-general. Another was under the orders of Condé, and the third was composed of the allied troops of Cologne and Munster, to which were added a certain number of French troops. The command of the last was given to the Duke of Luxembourg. All the troops which were in Lorraine and the neighbouring provinces marched between the 20th and 25th April to take up positions on the Sambre. The plan of operations had been much disputed. The Elector of Cologne, the Bishop of Munster, as well as the Bishop of Strasbourg, had strenuously demanded that the first enterprise should be the siege of Maestricht, where the Dutch had an enormous garrison. Condé also looked on the capture of this place as advantageous• to form a useful basis of operations. Turenne, on the other hand, put forward that as the

garrison amounted to 13,000 men the siege must be long
and difficult, and might discourage the French troops, and
give to the Dutch time to reorganize their forces and to be
joined by allies. On the other hand, he maintained that
this fortress might without inconvenience be left behind
by being masked, and that it was of advantage to bring
all the forces available on the Lower Rhine in order to
rapidly occupy the places and posts which might form
obstacles on the road to Amsterdam.

His plan was adopted. All the troops were, in the
early part of May, collected round Charleroy. On the
12th of that month the king marched thence upon Liege
and Viset, where provisions were assembled to be taken
to the Lower Meuse for the subsistence of the armies.
In the middle of May Turenne's army began operations
on this river. Maestricht was masked; Marseyk was
occupied to cut the communications between Holland
and Maestricht. The garrison of Maestricht was thus
made useless for the defence of the United Provinces,
and the French army was at the same time master of
the Meuse, which secured to it in case of retreat its
communications with France.

Lewis could thus commence in perfect security his
campaign of invasion. The first operation was to take
the places on the Lower Rhine, Rhineberg, Burich, Wesel,
and Rees, while the corps of Luxembourg on the right
would operate against Friesland. Fortress after fortress
fell in quick succession, and Lewis found himself master of
the Lower Rhine as far as its junction with the Wahl;
but as yet no blow had been struck against Holland itself,
for these towns, although garrisoned by Dutch troops,
belonged to the Electors of Brandenburg and Cologne.
To strike a death blow against the heart of the Dutch

M

administration and against the centre of the riches of the Republic it was necessary to pass either the Yssel or that part of the Rhine which still preserves the name of Rhine but soon afterwards takes that of Leck, and thus to open an avenue into the heart of Holland. The capture of the places situated in Dutch Brabant between the sea and the Rhine, such as Bergen-op-Zoom, Breda, and Bois Le Duc, would not have given access into the heart of the country. Their siege would have required much time, and allies, whom the States-General were striving to acquire, could arrive for their support. All the fortresses in front of the Rhine and Yssel surrendered. Some governors sent their keys at the sight of a single French squadron. Several officers fled from the towns where they were garrisoned before the enemy was near at hand.

Panic was general. The Prince of Orange had not enough troops to appear in the field. He hastily made lines behind the Yssel, and in them concentrated the principal forces of the Republic. Lewis might have crushed them by superior force by moving on the Yssel directly; but by crossing the Rhine he established his troops in the heart of the United Provinces. It was on the Rhine that Lewis directed his army, threatening the Yssel with a detachment. The army of Condé was chosen to make the passage. The people of the country told him that the peculiar dryness of the spring had made a ford on the arm of the Rhine near an old tower which served as a weighing-house, named Tolhuis. The river was 120 yards wide, and was fordable throughout, except for a distance of about twenty-five yards in its centre. On the 12th June, at daybreak, measures were taken to build a bridge of the boats invented by Martinet, protected by a battery. The Dutch general charged with defending the passage had

2,000 men but had no artillery. While the household troops of the French cavalry passed the river to the number of about 15,000 men, a few Dutch horsemen came into the water as if to oppose the passage, but these were struck by the guns on the right bank and could be of little effect. Condé crossed the river in a boat. The Dutch infantry was prepared to lay down its arms, and nobody in the French ranks would have been killed that day had it not been for the imprudence of the young Duke of Longue-ville. It is said that, with his head full of the fumes of wine, he fired his pistol on the enemy who were asking for quarter and killed one of their officers. The Dutch immediately seized their arms and fired a volley by which Longueville was killed. In the *mêlée* Condé's wrist was broken by a pistol ball, and he received the only wound which he ever received in any of his campaigns. Lewis crossed the river himself on the bridge. Such was the passage of the Rhine by Lewis, celebrated as one of the most glorious expeditions of his reign, and which really did not cost 200 men, but still dwells proudly in the memory of Frenchmen. The actual risk was little, but the result was considerable, since the passage forced the Prince of Orange to fall back from the Yssel, which could no longer serve as a barrier against invasion. The prince accordingly fell back upon Utrecht with about 12,000 men.

At Paris the passage of the river was loudly extolled. Its difficulty was greatly exaggerated. The air of grandeur which Lewis gave to all his actions, the rapidity of his conquests, the splendour of his reign, the idolatry of his courtiers, the taste of the French people, and especially the Parisians, for exaggeration, joined to their ignorance of war, made the passage of the Rhine to be considered a

prodigious military achievement. It was generally believed
that the whole army had crossed the river by swimming
in the presence of an intrenched enemy, and notwithstanding the artillery of an impregnable fortress called Tolhuis.

The Prince of Orange in falling back left some 16,000 or
17,000 men as garrisons of the fortresses on the Yssel, as
well as of Arnheim and Nimeguen, and was left with only
12,000 men. This dispersion of his army into fortresses
was a disastrous fault, and it seemed that the ruin of the
Republic was assured. While Lewis pressed on towards
Amsterdam, Luxembourg, moving by the Yssel, occupied
Groningen, Deventer, and Zntphen. Arnheim, Nimeguen,
Bommel, and some forty other fortresses fell. There was
hardly an hour in the day when the king did not receive intelligence of some new conquest. Utrecht sent in its keys (17th
June, 1672) and capitulated, with the whole of the province
which bears its name. Lewis entered the town triumphantly,
taking with him his confessor and the titular Archbishop
of Utrecht. The great church was solemnly taken back by
the Catholics, and the archbishop, who had hitherto borne
an empty title, was for a short time established in a real
dignity. The provinces of Utrecht, of Over Yssel and
Guelders, were subdued. The camp fires of the French were
seen from the top of the Stadhouse of Amsterdam. The
Jews established in that city hastily offered a friend of
Condé two millions of florins to secure them against pillage.
Naarden, a town near Amsterdam, was already taken.
Four horsemen marauding nearly seized Muyden, where
are the dykes which can inundate the country. This town
lies but some two miles from Amsterdam itself and is considered justly one of the keys of the capital. Holland
seemed lost, and the Prince of Orange suggested a scheme
which has an aspect of antique heroism. He told the

Dutch that even if their native soil and the marvels with which human industry covered it were buried under the ocean all was not lost. The Dutch might survive Holland. The shipping in its ports would carry 200,000 emigrants to the Dutch colonies, and there a new Dutch commonwealth might be reared beneath the Southern Cross with an exchange wealthier than that of Amsterdam, and Schools more learned than those of Leyden.

At the same time the military ability of Lewis was clouded, for although Turenne and Condé counselled him not to break up his army to form garrisons for the captured towns, Louvois contended that France had troops sufficient for both their garrisons and the field. Lewis believed, as is usually the case with princes, the minister who flattered rather than the soldiers who advised. Pressed at the very gates of their capital, the States-General sued for peace (28th June). Turenne and Colbert wished that their proposals should be accepted; Louvois persuaded Lewis to continue the war. Had the advice of Turenne been followed the frontier of France would have been carried to the Rhine, the road prepared for the union of the Spanish low countries with French territory, and six years of a terrible war been avoided, which cost the life of Turenne, and only finished at the end of 1678 by the treaty of Nimeguen, and on terms less advantageous to France than those proposed in 1672 by the United Provinces. The pride of Lewis and the haughtiness of Louvois can alone explain the insolent reply made on the 1st July to the terms proposed by the States. Another fault was also committed. The French had taken more than 30,000 Dutch prisoners. Condé proposed to employ them upon the public works of France, but Louvois released them at a ransom of two crowns per head. Thus

for an absurd sum a whole army was given back to the
Prince of Orange.' The terms offered by Lewis, which would
have reduced Holland almost to a state of servitude, were
rejected. The dykes were opened, the country inundated,
and an insurmountable barrier spread over the land in
front of the French armies. The whole country was turned
into a vast lake, from which the cities with their ramparts
and steeples rose like islands. The distress of Holland
roused the indignation of Europe. Sweden and the
Elector of Mayence wished to offer their mediation. The
English parliament urged Charles to take the part of the
Dutch. The Elector of Brandenburg and the emperor
united themselves against Lewis. Lewis himself returned
to enjoy the smiles of women and the praise of courtiers at
Versailles, and Turenne remained in Brabant with an
army of 20,000 men to complete the conquest.

It was decided that the French corps at Marseyk should
mask Maestricht more closely, and that Luxembourg with
a corps of from 18,000 to 20,000 men should watch the
country on the right of the Rhine. The tide now turned.
On the sea the result of the war had been doubtful, by
land the United Provinces obtained a respite, and a respite
was of immense importance. From every part of Germany
troops poured along the roads leading to the Rhine to support the Dutch against the French. Lewis found himself on
the point of a contest against half of Europe. In Holland
itself the French invasion produced terrible excitement
amongst the populace. The suffering and terrified people,
enraged against the government, in their madness attacked
the bravest captains and ablest generals. De Ruyter was
insulted by the mob. De Witt was torn in pieces before
the gate of the palace of the States-General at the Hague,
although he had governed the state for nineteen years

with virtue. With him perished his brother, who had served the Republic with his sword.

The inundation was more strenuously pursued. The country houses, which were numerous around Amsterdam, the villages and neighbouring cities of Leyden and Delft, were submerged. The peasants did not murmur to see their cattle drowned in their fields. Amsterdam, like a large fortress in the middle of the waters, was surrounded by vessels of war. Suffering was great. Fresh water was most difficult to obtain, but these extremities were preferred to French domination. For two years Holland remained submerged, and could be attacked only in winter and in frost. At the same time the States by energetic measures reorganized their armies and restored the Prince of Orange to the post which his family had held, that of Staatholder.

The succour that Holland merited was quickly provided by Europe, which armed for its defence. From Brandenburg and from Austria armies were hurrying up to the Rhine. Spain joined the cause. In Holland itself through the inundations the war was reduced on the part of the French to one of observation. Turenne remained with his army near Bois le Duc, but when he heard that the Emperor and Elector of Brandenburg were marching towards the Rhine he resolved to pass the river to stop them. The military strength of Lewis and the great name of Turenne made the Germans hesitate, and they moved with great circumspection. Turenne crosssed the Rhine (10th September) at Wesel and manœuvered to cover the river from Wesel to Coblenz. At the same time Condé arrived in Alsace with 18,000 men to guard the Upper Rhine, and a French corps of observation was left upon the Meuse.

At this time there commenced for Turenne a series of difficulties and trials, which came upon him from his own court much more than the enemy. During the last four years of his life, it was not Montecuculli who occupied his attention so much as it was Louvois, and the struggle was difficult for Turenne, since he had against him at the same time Lewis, Louvois, and Condé.

The allies undertook no serious steps before the middle of October, although at the beginning of that month they approached the Rhine, making a demonstration as if to attack Alsace and Lorraine. Turenne, convinced that their real object must be Holland, and that they would endeavour to join the Prince of Orange, particularly watched Cologne and Coblenz, and devoted his whole attention to barring the passage of the Rhine near those towns, while Lewis ordered him to move against the enemy and to fight. From Versailles Louvois, fidgety and meddlesome, laid down the smallest details of his movements, and thus sprang up the bitter correspondence between Louvois and Turenne which annoyed the marshal, and certainly hindered the thorough execution of his duty.

Thoroughly convinced that, at all cost, it was necessary to prevent the junction of the German armies with the Prince of Orange, he did not allow himself to be distracted by the feints of the enemy. The Germans crossed the Main ; Turenne did not send the reinforcements to Condé which the Prince asked for, since he was sure that Alsace and Lorraine were not seriously threatened. The bridge of Strasbourg, the only one by which the Confederates could cross the Rhine in that direction, had been destroyed by Condé. It was not near Strasbourg, but near Mayence, that the Germans did actually surprise (23rd November) the passage of the river.

They then thought that the road was clear by the
Electorate of Trèves towards Holland. They counted
without Turenne. He immediately moved his head-
quarters to Witlich, situated on the road from Maestricht
to Mayence, in the Electorate of Trèves, and thus took up
a position which prevented the Prince of Orange from
joining the Germans, and the Germans from marching
towards the Meuse without finding the French general, by
the simplest movement able to throw himself upon their
flanks if they attempted to pass either to the right or left.
His position left them no alternative but either to risk a
battle, in which case they ran every chance of complete
extermination, or to retire, since they could not remain in
a ravaged country. Retreat appeared to them preferable
to combat. Renouncing the left bank of the Rhine, they
repassed to the right, with the intention of establishing
themselves in the territory of the Elector of Cologne and the
Bishop of Münster, to oblige these two princes to renounce
their alliance with France. This showed that Turenne was
right in his previsions, since the Prince of Orange shortly
advanced with the hope of joining the Germans. He
traversed Brabant, brought his best troops beyond Maestricht, and arrived on the banks of the Roer, when he
heard of the retreat of the Confederates. Angered, he
wished to compensate himself by a bold stroke, and fell
upon Charleroy, which he besieged on the 15th December.
Should he succeed, the communication was cut between
France and its armies in Holland. Consternation was
great at court. Lewis hurried to Compiègne and made
Condé advance to succour the place, but an energetic sortie
forced the prince to retire on the 22nd December. The
conduct of Turenne in this campaign, which was violently
discussed in France, only merits praise. He had indirectly

defended Alsace and the left bank of the Rhine more
surely and certainly than by delivering battle, as was
demanded of him. Should he have won such a battle, he
would not have made the situation of the Germans more
unpleasant than it was in consequence of the retreat,
which cost them many men and very many horses. If he
had lost a battle, he must have withdrawn from the neighbourhood of Mayence, and retired to Alsace or Lorraine;
then the Germans would at their ease join the Dutch and
Spaniards in the Low Countries. Once more he had well
merited for France and Lewis the justice which the latter
afterwards rendered to him, and forced the allies to retire
across the Rhine and take up their winter quarters in
their own country.

At the time of the invasion of Holland France was at
the summit of her glory under Lewis. The name of his
generals impressed respect. His ministers were looked
upon as of superior genius to the counsellors of other
princes. Lewis was in Europe the only real king. The
Emperor Leopold was shut up at Vienna, and never appeared with his armies; Charles II. of Spain was emerging
from infancy; Charles II. of England was a lazy voluptuary.
The princes of Europe and their ministers made great mis-
takes. England acted in a contrary sense to all proper
principles by uniting with France to raise a power which
might be dangerous to herself. The emperor, the empire,
and the Spanish council did still worse in not opposing
at once the torrent of the French invasion. Lewis was
stayed by his own error, through not pursuing his easy
conquest with sufficient rapidity. Condé and Turenne
wished him to demolish some forty-five or fifty Dutch
fortresses which he had taken, to keep only five as store-
houses and points of communication, and to maintain his

army active in the field instead of disseminating it among
weak garrisons. Louvois gave contrary advice. Lewis
was more inclined to a war of sieges than to a war in
the field. The king missed the happy moment for marching into Amsterdam. He weakened his army by dividing
it into too many garrisons. He gave his enemy breathing
time. After the king left the army and returned to
France, affairs, as we have seen, changed. Turenne was
forced to march into Westphalia to bar the advance of
the Imperialists. The Spanish governor of Flanders, without being moved by the timid counsel of Spain, reinforced
the small army of the Prince of Orange with about 10,000
men. William could thus hold all in the balance until
the winter. Then a new war began. The inundations
were frozen over; the ice allowed the passage of armed
bodies. A French general made an attempt on Leyden
and on the Hague. A thaw came on. The places were
saved, and he and his troops exposed to much suffering
and great peril. In spite, Luxembourg committed some
considerable Dutch towns, which were well populated, to
the flames and pillage of the troops, and stained the
history of French war with indelible disgrace.

Everywhere the diplomatists of Lewis sought to prevent
alliances of foreign princes with the Dutch. There was
hardly a court where he had not influential pensioners.
Money was lavished on Charles II. to continue the war
against Holland, notwithstanding the anger of the English
people; Hungary was stirred up as a check on the movements of the cabinet of Vienna; still he could not prevent
the emperor and Spain from allying themselves with Holland and solemnly declaring war against France. The course
of French ambition had led to the Dutch, the natural allies
of France, becoming allies of the house of Austria.

CHAPTER XI.

FORMERLY the French had been unable to form a respectable naval contingent to the English fleet. In the year 1673 this was changed. Instead of thirty vessels, forty now took the sea under the lilies of France. The French officers had learnt facility of manœuvre from the English, with whom they had fought against the Dutch. The Duke of York, afterwards James II., Lord High Admiral, had invented the art of conveying orders on sea by the combinations of flags. Before then the French could not arrange a navy in battle. Their experience consisted in forcing one vessel against another, not acting in concert ; nor could they imitate on sea the movements of armies on land, in which separate corps support and secure each other. Their naval tactics were much the same as those observed by the Carthaginians or Romans. The result of naval reform was seen in June, when a three days' battle took place between the Dutch fleet, commanded by Ruyter, and the allied fleets of France and England.

On land, after the successes which Turenne had gained in the winter, Lewis wished to stay the war and distribute

his troops in winter quarters; but Turenne insisted on
driving the Germans beyond the district where they could
injure the allies of France, the Bishop of Münster and
the Elector of Cologne, who were loudly crying for aid,
and threatened in case of being deserted to abandon the
French alliance. With difficulty the minister and the
king were persuaded, but in January they gave a re-
luctant consent to the troops being moved. On the 25th
January Turenne crossed the Rhine at Wesel. The winter
was very severe. The ground was so hard that trenches
could not be opened before fortresses, but he conducted his
operations with a dash which resembled that of the campaign of Holland in the previous year. The Elector of
Brandenburg had invested Werl, which belonged to the
Elector of Cologne. Turenne raised the siege, and the
Elector fell back. Turenne pursued, pushed into the possessions of Brandenburg, and invested Unna, garrisoned
by 800 Prussians. The frost was too severe to allow of
trenches being dug, but the town was bombarded. In the
camp of the allies it was proposed to give battle, but there
were differences of counsel. The army was indeed drawn
up, but Turenne did not appear, and it was debated
whether he should be sought for. It was Sunday. The
opponents of fighting required the chaplain of the elector
to lengthen the service. He preached for three hours, and
his hearers had to decide in their minds whether it was
more disagreeable to be exposed to fire or to such a
lengthy discourse. Turenne still pushed forward; the
Elector of Brandenburg separated from the Imperialists; the Elector fell back on Lippstadt, the Imperialists
on Paderborn. Both retreated across the Weser and
passed the river at Minden, and took up quarters—the
Elector in the district of Minden, the Imperialists near

Hildesheim, and Turenne encamped on the Weser (7th of March).

All had gone well for the French in this campaign. Their moral force was enormous. A few dragoons had dispersed a German regiment. The French troops slept in the open, and sustained without any entrenchments the fire of musketry or of guns of besieged places. The men slept on the ground under snow. So severe was the cold that the principal medical officer reported that in a few days he cut off more than 2,000 of the soldiers' toes, but that they were so exhilarated with their victorious career that it made no difference in their marching. The retreat of the German army had been so painful that it now hardly mustered 22,000 men. The Dukes of Hanover and of Brunswick, who had understandings with France, were taking up arms. The Elector, doubtful of the earnest intentions of the Imperialists, and fearful for his own possessions in Westphalia, resolved to make peace with France. A treaty was signed (11th of April), by which he undertook not to aid, directly or indirectly, the enemies of Lewis, and his troops fell back into Brandenburg.

The Imperialists, after their departure, would not risk remaining alone on the Weser. Turenne crossed the Weser and drove them into Thuringia, whence they retired into Bohemia, while the troops of Lorraine, consisting of 4,000 horsemen, fell back on the Upper Rhine. Then only did the Marshal consent to give his troops rest between the Weser and the Rhine.

While Turenne was forcing the Elector of Brandenburg to make peace, Louvois was making dispositions for the summer campaign. Besides the armies of observation which he had in Roussillon and in Lorraine, he had 108,000 men to divide between Holland, Germany, and the Spanish low

countries.   New efforts were to be made to conquer
Holland.   Lewis counted mainly on the combined fleets of
France and England, which, by making a descent on the
Dutch coast, were to attack in reverse the line of defence of
the Prince of Orange, while Condé, in command of French
troops retained in Holland, threatened it in front with
35,000 men.   32.000 men under Lewis himself were
collected on the Lys to strike a blow there against the
Spanish low countries, or against Holland.   Turenne was
opposed to the emperor with 34,000 men, and was ordered
to remain beyond the Rhine to prevent the Republic being
aided by Austria, which was collecting a considerable army
in Bohemia, and had determined to act more energetically
than hitherto.

Lewis, having made the French seamen through the care
of Colbert, improved the art of the engineer by the industry of Vauban.   It was determined to besiege Maestricht.   Turenne's army was weakened for the purpose by
7,000 men, whom he sent without complaint, as he considered the conquest of Maestricht most important for the
interests of France.   It was defended by a brave governor
at the head of a garrison of 5,000 men.   Vauban, who
conducted the siege, used, for the first time in Europe,
parallels, which had been invented by Italian engineers in
the service of the Turks before Candia.   To these he added
places of arms made in the trenches where troops would be
held in readiness for action in case of sorties.   The siege
was strongly pushed, and Maestricht fell in eight days
(29th June, 1673).   Turenne took up a position near
Frankfurt, where he could prevent the Imperial army from
Bohemia moving towards the Rhine.   To cross the Main
he bought corn in Mayence and Frankfurt with the intention of keeping the boats which brought it to him.   He

got back the troops whom he had sent to the siege of
Maestricht after the place was taken, and established his
head-quarters at Wetzlar, where he remained till the 14th
August. This long occupation of Germany by idle troops
was unfavourable. The soldiers committed disorders in
neutral territory, and the German princes complained to
the king. Louvois sharply called upon Turenne to maintain more exact discipline, to which Turenne replied very
justly that the country was ruined as little as a country
could be when in the occupation of an army. Certainly
the valley of the Main did not suffer so much as did the
district of Trèves, when Lewis himself, marching from the
low countries to Lorraine, after the capture of Maestricht,
visited on this country the refusal of the Elector of Treves
to declare himself either an ally or enemy of France.
Trèves was taken on the 8th September. The French
cavalry was lodged on both sides of the Moselle at the
cost of the inhabitants. Saarbruck was occupied. Many
villages were burnt. Heavy contributions were levied for
the profit of the generals, and the Elector was driven for
refuge into Ehrenbreitsen. Nancy was taken. All the
inhabitants were forced to work and give money for com-
pleting the fortifications. All the neighbouring buildings,
even the most revered churches, were thrown down. This
ill-treatment roused Germany against France, for the
Elector of Trèves addressed to the diet a letter on the
miseries of his country, and on the 30th August, treaties
were concluded at the Hague with the United Provinces by
the Duke of Lorraine, Spain, and the Emperor. At the
same time Lewis was checked (14th September) in Holland.
The Prince of Orange retook Naarden. William, who had
only officers without zeal and soldiers without courage, had
been obliged to exact stern military discipline, and execute

those who abandoned their post. Lewis, although French officers required no such example, was equally severe. Dupas, a brave man, surrendered Naarden. It is true that he only held it four days, while the regulations declared that he should have stood three assaults, but only given up the town after a contest of five hours. The king, however, ordered him to be sentenced to death and his sword broken. Turenne interceded, and obtained for Dupas permission to enter Grave, where he served as a volunteer, and died nobly a year afterwards when that town was besieged.

The genius of Vauban, the care of Louvois, the experience of Turenne, the dash of Condé—could not repair the fault committed in the previous year of dissipating the French troops into garrisons, weakening the army, and failing to occupy Amsterdam. Condé in vain tried to pierce the heart of the inundated low countries. Turenne himself failed in preventing the junction of the Imperialists under Montecuculli and the Prince of Orange at the end of August. He advanced to Aschaffenburg with the intention of moving against the Imperialists and throwing them back into Bohemia. To execute this design, reinforcements were indispensable, and he asked for them.

Lewis, who expected a declaration of war from Spain, and wished to conquer Franche-Comte, was holding back his troops for this dearly-loved enterprise, and held useless at Nancy a corps which, sent in time to Germany, might have led to decisive successes.

Lewis recognised the advantage of Turenne's offensive plans, but since he declined to send the necessary reinforcements proposed to him to be contented to take up a defensive position on the Tauber, a southern affluent of the Main, at an almost equal distance between Philipsburg

N

and Nuremberg.   In the view of the king this was all
that was necessary to prevent Montecuculli from reaching
the Rhine and joining the Prince of Orange, while the
idea of Turenne was to drive the enemy away from ap-
proaching the Rhine.   The quarrel between Louvois and
Turenne increased, although the marshal pointed out that
his army was perishing—that his battalions hardly mustered 350 men, that his English and Irish soldiers were
fading away, that the regiments from Holland were feeble,
and that more than 500 men had deserted near Frankfort,
and that his whole force amounted to barely 13,000.   The
army of the emperor, which had been slowly concentrated
at Egra, mustered 25,000 men, and was under the command
of Montecuculli, who had only accepted the charge on condition of being untrammeled by any orders from the
Austrian ministry.   The object of Montecuculli was to
reach the lower Rhine, join the Prince of Orange and
the Spaniards, force the Elector of Cologne and the Bishop
of Munster to renounce their alliance with France ; and
finally to drive the French from Holland.   To deceive
Turenne he made a feint of wishing to invade Lorraine
and Alsace, marched from Egra at the end of August,
and crossed the high Palatinate in three columns, which
united near Nuremburg (3rd September).

   The direction of this march caused Turenne to pass to
the left of the Main, especially since the orders of the
court told him to bar the road to Alsace (6th September).
On pushing southwards he learnt that the Imperialists were
establishing their bakeries at Marienthal.   Wishing to
anticipate then at this point which would have opened
to them the roads to the Upper Rhine, he marched in
the night and seized the place.   Montecuculli marched
the same day to Furth.   His intention was to draw the

French away from the Maine by threatening their right
flank, and feigned to wish to establish himself on the upper
course of the Tauber. He moved on Rothenburg. His
army, reinforced by troops of Saxony and Lorraine, now
consisted of 40,000 men. Turenne had seized all the
passages of the Main, except that of Wurtzburg, of which
the bishop had promised to maintain neutrality. At this
moment Montecuculli could advance neither on Holland
nor on Alsace without exposing his flank to the French
army.

Turenne would have done well to have remained in this
position, and not to have trusted the word of any man for
guarding the important passage of Wurtzburg, which,
under the circumstances, he ought himself to have secured. Montecuculli corrupted the bishop, moved to
Wurtzburg, gained its bridge, and there crossed the
Maine, thus turning the extreme left flank of Turenne,
who only succeeded in taking some baggage and stores
from the rear-guard.

Montecuculli thus threatened Turenne's communications
with Frankfurt and the rich country around that town
from which he drew his supplies. He seized some of the
French magazines. The perfidy of the prelate had given
great advantage to the Germans. Masters of the right
bank of the Main, they held the key of Frankfurt, the
richest country of Germany for corn.

Turenne was obliged, for the sake of supplies, to fall
back upon the Tauber, where he had magazines. This retreat opened immediately to the enemy the road to the
lower Rhine. He would have done better to have retreated at once by Aschaffenburg or Frankfurt, for he
must have known that the real object of the Imperialists
must be to join with the Prince of Orange, and not

unsupported to invade Alsace, where they would have been
met by Condé with 20,000 troops.

Montecuculli marched down the Main, little molested by
Turenne, whose army was much exhausted. The Imperialist
general wished, however, before striking for his junction
with the Prince of Orange, to force Turenne over the Rhine.
With this object he menaced the French communications
with Philipsbourg, which had now become Turenne's base.
He pretended to cross the Main, near Frankfurt (17th
October).

Turenne was deceived, did not remain close enough to
his enemy, fell back towards Philipsburg, leaving the
Tauber. In this retreat there was great misery; famine
was frightful; the French soldiers plundered their magazines, deserted in masses, so that Turenne could not follow
sufficiently closely the movements of the enemy, but he
himself acknowledges that he was surprised by the rapidity
with which Montecuculli pushed down the Main. The
Germans moved rapidly from Frankfurt to Mayence, began to build a bridge below this town, and pushed 5,000
or 6,000 men into the lower Palatinate. This alarmed
Turenne for Treves, to which the Imperialists were
already nearer than the French. His uneasiness on account of Treves forced Turenne over the Rhine to the
neighbourhood of Neustadt and Kaiserlautern, where he
took up a position from which he could secure Treves and
guard Alsace. He foresaw that the Dutch, the Spaniards,
and the Imperialists uniting might take Bonn, and so gain
a safe communication between Germany and Holland, but
he was unable to move to the neighbourhood of Cologne on
account of want of provisions.

It was upon Bonn that the allies moved. William,
warned of the march of Montecuculli, assembled in Brabant

20,000 Dutch, to which Spain, who had just declared war with France, added 6,000.   This army could either join the Imperialists on the Lower Rhine, or invade French Flanders.

Lewis covered this province with 14,000 men at Oudenarde under Condé, who would have found it under any circumstances difficult with inferior forces to hold the frontier, but William directed his operations in another direction.   He marched from Brabant to the Meuse, which he crossed at Venlo (22nd October), and continued his march to Coblenz to join Montecuculli.

Condé, unable to oppose this manœuvre, remained on the Scheldt to keep down the Spanish garrisons, and could only send 9,000 infantry to annoy William.   The Elector of Treves, who had promised neutrality, quickly broke his word, and allowed the Imperialists to use the bridges of Coblenz over the Rhine and Moselle.   This advantage was decisive, and gave Montecuculli the greatest facility of communication.   He became, in fact, master of the greater part of the lower Rhine.   The passage of Coblenz was equally valuable to him, whether he wished to march on the Palatinate, or against Philipsburg.   In the meantime he embarked his infantry in boats on the Rhine, and sent them down the river towards Bonn, where he joined with the Dutch, and the siege of Bonn was undertaken by the united allied army, while some cavalry on the Moselle watched Turenne.   Bonn quickly fell.   The fortifications were bad, the magazines ill provided, and the garrison very weak.   Its fall was a great blow to the French, for Bonn cut their communications with Holland, which they were obliged to abandon, and deprived Lewis of his two allies, the Elector of Cologne and the Bishop of Munster, who, under threat of being placed under the ban of the empire, were obliged to make peace with the Dutch.

In this campaign Montecuculli entirely out-manœuvred Turenne. This may have been due to want of reinforcements, which Lewis refused to him, and particularly to the want of provisions, of which he bitterly complained; but the latter excuse cannot be accepted on behalf of any general, for the duty of a general is as much to provide his troops with provisions as it is to provide them with advantageous posts in battle.

Turenne could make no endeavour to raise the siege of Bonn. The season was bad, the roads were wretched, provisions were wanted, the troops were fatigued and must have rest. The soldiers had to be separated into winter quarters (19th December), for the officers commanding regiments reported that a march of twenty miles at that time would have destroyed the army more than the loss of a battle. The men were distributed—some near Treves, some on the Sarre; two corps were sent into Alsace and Lorraine, and some wintered in Burgundy. Montecuculli returned to Vienna, giving the command of his army to the duke of Bournonville (28th November). His troops were cantoned in the electorate of Cologne and duchy of Juliers, on the left of the Rhine, and some of his cavalry on the right of the river as far as Minden. The Prince of Orange returned to Holland, and the Spaniards to the low countries, where they occupied Dinant, Namur, and Huy. The enemies of Lewis now commanded the whole country from the Meuse to the Weser.

CHAPTER XII.

THE parliament of England urged Charles to make peace with Holland, and expressly declared that no more supplies should be granted for the war unless the enemy distinctly refused to consent to reasonable terms. Charles found it necessary to postpone to a more convenient season all thought of executing the treaty of Dover, and had to pretend to return to the policy of the triple alliance. Temple was called from his books and his flowers to conclude a separate peace with the United Provinces, and again became ambassador at the Hague, where his presence was regarded as a sure pledge for the sincerity of the court of St. James. This and the capture of Bonn made Lewis quit the three Dutch provinces which he held, with as much rapidity as he had conquered them. It was not, however, without some result that he returned from the province of Utrecht, which was heavily fined; but the triumphal arch at the gate of Saint Denis and other monuments of Dutch conquests were hardly completed when the conquest was already abandoned. The result of the short triumph of France in the United Provinces was a bloody war against Spain, Germany, and Holland.

The grandeur of the French monarch rose with his danger. The wisdom of his government and the force of his state appeared greater when it was necessary for him to defend himself against so many leagued powers and against great generals more than when he had taken French Flanders and the half of Holland from enemies unable to defend themselves.

The failures of the previous campaign roused up enemies against France. The Elector Palatine and the Duke of Brunswick joined their troops to those of the empire. Later, the Elector of Brandenburg also joined against France. The Electors of Bavaria and of Hanover were the only German princes remaining neutral. Condé and Turenne were consulted on the plan of the campaign, and Lewis himself had to intervene to make Louvois treat his generals with courtesy and civility. A judicious and simple plan was formed. Holland was to be abandoned except Grave, which was to hold the stores captured in the fortresses that must be abandoned. The line of the Rhine, which the capture of Bonn did not allow longer to be held advantageously, was to be given up, but the course of the Meuse from the French frontier to Maestricht was to be strongly held. Alsace and Lorraine were to be covered against the Germans, Roussillon against the Spaniards, and the offensive was to be vigorously taken in Flanders and in Franche-Comte. An absolute king has great advantages over other kings when his finances are well administered. Lewis was able to furnish an army of about 23,000 men to Turenne ·against the Imperialists, one of 40,000 to Condé against the Prince of Orange. A large body of troops was on the frontier of Roussillon. A fleet, laden with soldiers, carried the war against the Spaniards even to Messina, while Lewis himself marched to make

himself master a second time of Franche-Comte.   In April
he entered that province, and Spain, with reason and
entreaty, solicited the Swiss to allow a passage for its
troops to aid it. Lewis advanced more solid arguments. His
ready money caused the passage to be refused, Besançon
was besieged. Vauban directed the attack. The town was
taken in nine days, and at the end of six weeks all Franche-
Comte was subdued.   It has ever since remained annexed
to France, a monument of the weakness of the Spanish
ministry, and of the strength of that of Lewis.

Turenne meanwhile had to observe the allies on the
Rhine, and to cover Franche-Comte from any attack.   His
fortresses were in a bad state of repair, and his army was
small enough to watch the course of the Rhine from Basle
to Coblenz.   He strongly occupied Haguenau and Saverne
to guard the north of Alsace, and sent a strong detachment
to Belfort, which prevented the Duke of Lorraine, who
was forced to retreat (15th May), from making a raid into
the southern part of the province.   The Germans made an
endeavour to gain the bridge of Strasbourg, but were
prevented by the vigilance of Turenne.   They then moved
towards Heidelberg to join the Palatine troops and those
of the emperor which the Duke of Bournonville was bringing from the neighbourhood of Cologne.   Turenne was
determined to prevent this junction, and to take his
adversaries in detail before they could effect it.   He had
only 6,000 horses, 3,000 infantry, and 6 guns, but he
advanced across the Rhine against the enemy, who fell
back towards Heilbron on the news of his advance, to be
covered by the Neckar.   Turenne came up with Caprara,
who commanded the force at Sitenzheim (16th June), where
he attacked it in a strong position and cannonaded it
heavily while it was without artillery.   His infantry were

then called into action. A narrow defile was stormed,
and the Imperialists were driven off the field, and with
difficulty effected their retreat to Heidelberg and Heilbron,
followed, as far as the Neckar, by a detachment of French
cavalry which made many prisoners. Caprara lost also
2,000 men who were killed in the battle. He made an
error in fighting at Sitenzheim; he ought to have fallen
back and waited his junction with Bournonville before
engaging. Turenne determined to prevent the junction of
the Germans with the duke, and though his resolution may
appear at first sight hazardous, it was necessary that he
should engage them before they were joined by larger
reinforcements. The result of his victory was that the
allied troops near Cologne, who were to march to Flanders,
had to be recalled and sent to the Rhine to aid the Duke
of Lorraine. If the French army had not been fatigued
by the series of marches which had lasted for several
months, the victory might have been decisive; but
Turenne was obliged to give rest to his troops, and fell
back across the Rhine to Neustadt in the Palatinate to
refresh his army. The Imperialists collected the remains
of their forces beyond the Neckar where Bournonville
joined them. They could not resume the offensive, and
they camped between Heidelberg and Mannheim. Here
Turenne again advanced against them (3rd July). They
were entrenched and fortified, covered by the Neckar, and
their army mustered 16,000 men; the marshal had only
11,000. He wished to drive them away from the Rhine,
and resolved to attack them. Hardly had the action
begun when they broke up hurriedly from their intrenchments, and retired behind the Maine in the direction of
Frankfurt, throwing away, in the precipitation of their
flight, cuirasses, arms, and equipment.

This flight made Turenne master of the Palatinate. He there distributed his troops and allowed them to live upon the country for a month, consume all the forage and all the harvest, so as to prevent any other troops from being able to live there that year. This wasting of the Palatinate has remained as a stain on the memory of Turenne. The elector from his palace in Mannheim could see the flames of it is said twenty-six villages at one time, and hear the cries of his subjects, whose throats were being cut for not granting contributions to the army. He sent a challenge to Turenne to fight a duel, which was declined.

It does not appear, however, why this harrying of the Palatinate should be so strongly insisted upon as a disgrace. War is an odious thing, but if war is to be made it must be made without regard to the conveniences of the inhabitants, and the more terrible and horrible it is made the less likelihood of war. Had Turenne not wasted the country, troops could constantly have moved into it and subsisted there, who could at their ease have attacked his positions at Haguenau and Saverne, or Philipsburg. If he should be called to defend the upper Rhine, it was necessary for him, with the small force at his command, to take every measure that he could, to prevent the advance of a superior enemy upon him at various points, and wasting the country is always legitimate for defensive purposes. It is hardly possible to destroy the resources of a country without great cruelty to the inhabitants, for the only measure by which these can be compelled to yield up their supplies is by fire and sword when requisitions are not complied with. Turenne wasted a hostile country. It must be remembered that an English army in order to compel Massena to fall back from Lisbon, wasted a friendly country and thus turned the tide of the Peninsular war. Frederick the Great laid down the rule that the inhabitants of a conquered country should be threatened with fire and sword if they do not furnish, when required, the supplies demanded from them. Such terrible exactions for military purposes will continue so long as war is made. The responsibility rests not on the soldier who carries out military operations, but on the ministry that brings about war.

The Germans made new levies and new concentrations, and appeared so formidable that Lewis actually contemplated retiring into Lorraine and evacuating all Alsace, with the exception of Brisach and Philipsburg. Against this plan Turenne strongly remonstrated, and took up his position near Landau, in the Palatinate on the French side of the Rhine, where he consumed the provisions nearly as effectually as on the further side. Bournonville collected a large army of Germans, and without waiting the arrival of the great elector, who was also coming up, passed the Rhine at Mayence with 30,000 men and thirty guns (28th and 29th August).

Louvois was much alarmed. Turenne was perfectly cool at Landau. Alsace lay behind him, and the enemy could not push along the road to France without exposing his communications. Thus the marshal indirectly covered Paris—directly Alsace. This Bournonville recognised and felt he must march against Turenne, but he found him so strongly posted that he dared not attack. His army suffered from want of forage, and he had again to cross the Rhine (20th September), nor did he dare to besiege Philipsburg with Turenne so close at hand, but marched by the Rhine on the right bank to approach Strasbourg.

Turenne quickly sent to prevent the magistrates of that

free town from breaking their neutrality and allowing the Imperialists to pass the Rhine at their bridge. He followed with the remainder of his army, and when he came near Strasbourg found that the magistrates had been gained over by the emissaries of the emperor, and had given up their bridge.

The French government had made a great fault in not seizing Strasbourg, and holding the passage over the Rhine there. Napoleon lays this fault upon Turenne, but it would have been a grave responsibility for a general in command to adopt such a course which would appear to fall within the province of the government, not of the executive officer (24th of September).

The imperialists gained Strasbourg, and detachments of their troops poured into high Alsace. The elector of Brandenburg arrived on the Neckar with thirty-two guns. Turenne was in a country without supplies. He had to defend France open to invasion—to cover many places in Alsace, and if he lost any time, the junction of the elector with Bournonville would permit the allies to throw 50,000 men on the road to Paris. The situation was critical. Turenne resolved to prevent the junction as he had prevented at the opening of the campaign that of Bournonville and Caprara. Bournonville had crossed the river by the bridge of Strasbourg, and was encamped near that town. Turenne attacked him at Entzheim. The imperial left rested on a wood which was the important tactical point of the field. Turenne assailed it with heavy forces. Twice it was taken ; twice the French were driven out. A third attack was successful, but in the meantime the centre and left of the French line had been weakened by the withdrawal of troops to support the attack against the woods. Turenne had also committed an error by scattering detach-

ments of infantry amongst his cavalry, which made his
cavalry lose its mobility, and left his infantry without support when the horsemen advanced. When the French
cavalry moved forward, Bournonville made a brilliant
manœuvre to outflank the French left.; but the French
troops fought well and saved it. Had Turenne, when he
found the wood strongly held, and had to direct heavy
masses upon it, moved his army under cover of the forces
attacking the wood boldly to the right, he might have
enveloped the Austrian left flank, and made the victory
more decisive than it was.

As it was he gained the day, but no great advantage.
He could not pursue, and both armies had to fall back to
the positions they had held before the battle. The French
lost 2,000 men, the Germans 3,000, but their army was
only weakened, not destroyed. It was still in Alsace, and
the elector was coming up. The danger threatening France
was still grave.

Although his army was suffering from want, Turenne
was not willing to abandon Alsace to the Germans. He
fell back upon his positions near Haguerau and Saverne,
where he could protect his communications with Philipsburg, and also operate against the flank of the allies if they
should advance into Lorraine. These slowly followed him,
but without the impulse which a concentrated command
gives. In their councils of war their generals could not
agree as to the operations to be undertaken. After much
indecision they fell back under the protection of Strasbourg.
Turenne himself with his small force was able to do nothing.
The Germans, deceived by his inaction, thought that the
campaign was over, and distributed, at the end of November,
their army into winter quarters which extended from
Belfort along the Vosges to Colmar and Schlestadt.

Turenne now undertook the most brilliant manœuvre that he had ever contemplated. After having allowed his enemies to believe that he gave up disputing with them the possession of Alsace, and making dispositions at Haguenau and Saverne, as if he were fortifying these places to protect garrisons which he was about to abandon in a hostile country, while he himself retired into Lorraine at the end of December, he crossed the Vosges, and descended into Lorraine, leaving only six French regiments in Haguenau and Saverne; but his object was not to withdraw into Lorraine. He moved rapidly, covered by the Vosges, southwards. The march was painful; snow fell in abundance, the brooks and rivers overflowed, the roads sunk; but a frost coming on hardened the roads, and on the 29th of December all his troops were assembled at Belfort, which was the place appointed for the rendezvous. Then he burst into Alsace, driving the scattered detachments of the enemy in front of him in general flight. The allies endeavoured to assemble their dispersed corps beyond the Ill, and resolved to dispute the passage of that river, to give the main body of their army time to concentrate at Colmar. Turenne followed them closely. He saw that the success of his enterprise depended upon diligence. He marched upon the Ill, cutting off many of the allied garrisons who had not time to retire. Sharply pressed, the allies fell back on Colmar. Turenne pushed on, capturing many stragglers, and on the 5th of January, in three columns, bore down upon the elector, who had massed between 30,000 and 40,000 between Colmar and Turckheim. The German position was well chosen. Its flanks were covered by the Fecht and the Ill, and its front by a canal communicating between the two rivers. The left of the elector was on Colmar, his right towards Turckheim;

but his troops were not sufficient to extend to that town,
and he had only placed there 300 dragoons. Turenne,
seeing that Turckheim commanded the plain, notwithstanding the difficulty of the ground, moved towards that
place over some spurs of the Vosges, carried the town, and
captured the dragoons. Then, he turned the right flank of
the elector, who in vain endeavoured, seeing too late the
importance of the place, to retake Turckheim. The
fighting was sharp. Turenne had a horse wounded under
him, but the Germans were finally driven off and forced to
retreat. In the night they retired on Schlestadt. Turenne
occupied Colmar. The Imperialists retreated by Strasbourg
across the Rhine, and there was soon left in Alsace no
Germans, except the wounded and dead, and one small
garrison, which was taken in a few days. Turenne then
spread his army into the winter quarters which they had
so well deserved, and the French, who had strong garrisons
at Brisach and Philipsbourg, put under contribution the
whole of the country on the right of the Rhine from the
frontiers of Basle to the Neckar. During the whole of this
long campaign, Turenne, with much fewer troops than the
enemy, had supported an offensive and defensive war, had
discerned and defeated all the projects of his adversaries,
beaten the allies each time they attacked, and closed the
road into France to their battalions which were greedy to
invade it. He showed all the activity in which they failed,
and, profiting by their tardiness, prevented them from
entering Lorraine and Franche-Comte. He drove them
out of Alsace by the display of the most brilliant military
talent, and established his reputation as the first strategist
of the day.

CHAPTER XIII.

CAMPAIGN OF 1675.

FRANCE, thanks to the heroic labours of Turenne, had the advantage over its enemies in the campaign of 1674. At the beginning of 1675 the coalition, beaten everywhere, had need of time to repair its disasters, and its forces diminished in number at the very time when they became most necessary. The Swedes renewed their alliance with France, and interfering in the north of Germany, attacked the States of the Elector of Brandenburg, who had to withdraw his army from the Rhine to defend his own possessions. The Dutch appeared desirous of peace. In the Mediterranean the Spanish fleet went down before the French, and the town of Messina recognised Lewis XIV. as its sovereign. Louvois at the same time increased his troops, and by calling out the ban and the arriere ban, raised a large fund from the tax insisted upon from those who were unwilling to serve in person. Thus, at the beginning of the year, Lewis was able to put into the field on the northern frontier an army of nearly 70,000 men, with which, in the beginning of May, he determined to undertake the siege of Limbourg. Turenne was again placed in Alsace to watch the Imperialists. The Emperor,

o

no longer trusting to princes as generals, placed Montecuculli in command of 12,000 infantry and 14,000 cavalry to
oppose Turenne, who, in May, collected an army of about
25,000 men near Schlestadt. The two first strategists of
the day were now pitted against each other. Each endeavoured to spare his own country from being the theatre
of war, and to throw the burden upon that of his adversary. Montecuculli quickly moved from Ulm, and the
same day as Turenne quitted Paris after taking leave of
the King to join his army, the German general marched
rapidly on Strasbourg, and began to negotiate with the
magistracy for a passage over their bridge. Turenne
reached Schlestadt on the 19th of May, immediately started
with his cavalry, and advanced within sight of the
ramparts of Strasbourg. The people had already been
gained by the money of the emperor, but the presence of
Turenne prevented the engagement being carried out.

Montecuculli did not, however, abandon the idea of
passing the river. He knew that it was only the presence of the French that prevented Strasbourg from declaring in his favour. If he could only draw Turenne
away he might succeed. With this object he made a
feint as if to besiege Philipsburg. Turenne was content to send a detachment to reinforce the garrison, but
still held near Strasbourg. To be able in case of attack to
approach Philipsburg by either bank of the Rhine, and to
make Montecuculli uneasy for Freibourg, he made a bridge
of boats near Ottenheim, about six miles from Strasbourg.
Montecuculli, in hopes that if he crossed the Rhine and
threatened to invade France, Turenne would withdraw from
Strasbourg, crossed at Spire on the 1st June, and pushed
his light troops towards Landau to threaten the Moselle,
spreading the report that he was about to seek Turenne, in

order to give him battle. Again the marshal was not duped. He would not move. Montecuculli, after remain-ing for a few days beyond the Rhine, had to recross, not daring by an advance to leave his rear and lines of com-munication open to attack.

Turenne then turned the tables, and himself crossed the stream by his bridge at Ottenheim, and advanced down the left bank of the river to prevent Montecuculli from estab-lishing flying bridges below Strasbourg. In vain Monte-cuculli manœuvred against the right flank of the French in order to endeavour to cut them off from their bridge. His manœuvres were aided by the fact that Turenne had placed his bridge so far from Strasburg, and thus had two important points to defend, while if he had placed his bridge nearer the town, the objective of the enemy's at-tack would have been decreased, but Turenne kept pressing forwards, and bearing his weight against the Austrian left, at length placed Montecuculli in such a position that he must either retire or be driven into the Rhine.

The German general naturally preferred the former course. His army, covered by the rear guard, which was to hold some small intrenchments, began to move towards the Black Forest. Turenne prepared to attack him in his retreat. Turenne ordered his movements to be care-fully watched by a general officer, who sent two officers to beg him to go himself to observe the march of the enemy. A third message, brought by Lord Hamilton, made him mount his horse and move to his right wing, where he met Saint Hilare, a general of artillery, on a hill, and went to join him. Saint Hilare was pointing out to him the enemy's column, when two small guns in the Austrian works fired—one of the balls carried off the left arm of Saint Hilare, and struck Turenne on his left side. His horse, frightened, turned round and moved off some twenty paces, when the marshal fell off dead. When Saint Hilare's son, who was present, saw his father wounded, he burst into tears, but the general said, "It is not for me you should weep, but for this great man."

Thus died this great man when he was preparing a stroke which might have done much to finish the war which still endured for three years longer. He left to France a great memory, to Europe a glorious name, to all soldiers a noble study, to all men a grand example.

Turenne was mourned both by his soldiers and the people. Lewis recognised his worth and his services. His body was embalmed on the battle-field, near the Sassbach, and was taken to Paris, where it was buried with great pomp, in the cathedral of Saint Denis, in the chapel of the Bourbons. Here it rested until the revolution, when, with those of the kings and queens of France, it was torn up. It was found to be so perfectly embalmed, that the features were distinctly recognised. For some time the body was kept by a sacristan, and shown for a small fee to any visitors. It was then taken to the museum of the Garden of Plants, and was finally conveyed with great pomp during the reign of the first Napoleon to the Invalides, where it now rests.

Turenne was not always successful in war. He was beaten at Marienthal, Rethel, and Cambrai. He had faults, and he was great enough to acknowledge them. He did not make brilliant conquests, and he did not, as a rule, deliver great battles, the result of which may make one nation master of another; but he always repaired his defeats. He did much with small resources, and he was renowned as the greatest captain of Europe at a time when the art of war was more studied than it had ever been before. His defection in the wars of the Fronde was a reproach to him. He was believed to be on terms of more than friendship with Madame de Longueville. He exercised in the Palatinate cruelties which are stated not to have been necessary, yet he preserved the reputation of a good man, wise and moderate, because his virtues and his great talents, his humility, his modesty, his self-denial, his care for his soldiers, and his tenderness for others, made men forget his frailties, and the faults which he had in common with others of mankind.

It would be not only dishonest but unwise to regard Turenne as a perfect hero or an infallible soldier, yet he probably approached more nearly to the heroic and more nearly to infallibility than any other captain who has ever drawn sword ; nor would it be honest to deny that in private life he was not without stain, although it must also be acknowledged that his private life was far superior to the private life of most men of that day when gambling, debauchery, and amours were considered the main occupations and proper pursuits of the gentleman. Too great virtue cannot be expected even in the noblest examples of humanity. It would repel many, would irritate many, and would be unnatural to mankind.

If he is to be compared with any of the great generals of the centuries which had passed before his time, he probably more resembles Gonzalvo of Cordova, named the Great Captain, than any other. And if he be compared with those who followed him, his integrity, his honesty, and his modesty put him more upon a par with Wellington than with most other generals.

What happened in Alsace immediately after the death of Turenne made his loss the more marked. Montecuculli, who had been held in check by the marshal for three months, beyond the Rhine, passed that river so soon as he knew Turenne could no longer oppose him.

Montecuculli, on hearing of his death from a deserter, immediately said, "A man has died who was a glory to mankind."

THE END.

LONDON : R. CLAY, SONS, AND TAYLOR, PRINTERS.

CPSIA information can be obtained at www.ICGtesting.com
Printed in the USA
LVOW071832310512

284041LV00003B/19/A